write what should not be forgotten

—isabel allende

The Art of the Essay

from ordinary life
to extraordinary words

*includes activities for personal journals,
classrooms, and writing groups!*

c h a r i t y   s i n g l e t o n   c r a i g

Masters in fine living series

ts T. S. Poetry Press • New York

T. S. Poetry Press
Ossining, New York
Tspoetry.com

© 2019, Charity Singleton Craig

Cover image by L.L. Barkat

ISBN 978-1-943120-30-7

Library of Congress Cataloging-in-Publication Data:
Craig, Charity Singleton
    [Nonfiction/Writing/Essays.]
    The Art of the Essay:
        From Ordinary Life to Extraordinary Words—
        includes activities for personal journals, classrooms,
        and writing groups! (Masters in Fine Living Series)
    ISBN 978-1-943120-30-7
    Library of Congress Control Number: 2019907709

to my parents, micky costin and marshall singleton,
for always encouraging me to try

—charity singleton craig

Contents

Let Me Introduce You

What kind of writer are *you*?

For years, I wasn't sure how to answer that question, though I experimented in what essayist Brian Doyle called the "widest fattest most generous open glorious honest endlessly expandable form of committing prose" without realizing my own secret. Wasn't I simply engaging in first-person explorations of the everyday topics of my world? And, when I responded to ideas and quotes (as though the authors I captured them from really cared what I thought), wasn't this just an article, a blog post, a story? Surely these weren't essays—those serious three-part, five-paragraph school assignments, or the erudite think pieces published in magazines and journals. What I wrote was just, well, ordinary.

How about you? Do you have an essay secret, too?

"There's nothing ordinary," said one speaker, at a writers conference I attended several years ago. "If you pay close enough attention, you will find something miraculous, extraordinary. The world is everywhere whispering essays."

I almost missed this, I thought, as Patrick Madden, associate professor of English at Brigham Young University, and Brian Doyle, then the editor of *Portland Magazine*, discussed essays in a session I'd nearly overlooked because of its mysterious title: "The Magpie Form." But when Madden described essays as "recreating an experience and thinking about it," and Doyle talked about essayists as "story-catchers" gathering up "shards of holiness," my secret revealed itself.

I am an essayist. You might be, too.

A few months after the Magpie session, I heard Scott Russell Sanders speak about his writing life and process, at an event I attended with my friend and colleague Ann Kroeker. Sanders shared from his memoir *A Private History of Awe*. As he read about a childhood moment when his father took him out on the covered porch during a thunderstorm, I noticed Ann jot in her journal, "I want to write like that."

I shifted to the edge of my seat. Sanders had, as a young boy, sitting amidst the stacks at the public library, fallen in love with the "miraculous power of language, whether written or spoken." Books ushered him into a life otherwise out of reach, where he could "follow any question wherever it led, and all for free."

Writing essays affords you the same miraculous privilege. You can explore questions, follow them to an ending, even if it isn't always a conclusion. You can pursue the very heart of what it means to write essays: *to try*.

That's what French writer Michel de Montaigne, who is thought to have birthed the essay form, called his own writing: *essais*, or "attempts." After the death of his dear friend, humanist poet Étienne de la Boétie, Montaigne left behind an elite career in law and politics to isolate himself with words. He entered the tower of his family estate for what became a ten-year self-imposed exile, during which he wrote about a character he described as "Myself." In each carefully crafted treatment of subjects others might consider mundane, he recognized that the "Myself" character emerging from his work was simply a temporary construction, and, writes *New Yorker* essayist Jane Kramer, "nothing he wrote about himself was likely to apply for much longer than it took the ink he used, writing it, to dry."

As 21st-century citizens well acquainted with constructed selves, like those we profess on social media or present in person in our compartmentalized lives, this sounds like a perfectly modern, if not self-indulgent, approach to writing. But according to Kramer, "However you read them, Montaigne's books were utterly, if inexplicably, original." Other autobiographies of the day employed more narrative or confessional techniques. Montaigne's writings were like conversations between himself and the writers on his shelf.

But is today's essay the same form that was birthed by Montaigne in the sixteenth century?

Professor Madden, co-leader of that Magpie session discussed before, wonders whether the term *essay* "has been largely hijacked and adulterated beyond recognition." He blames school writing assignments that have co-opted the term, but he also implicates the bevy of creative nonfiction writers (memoirists, travel writers, and new journalists) whose writing might be good but "often essays nothing, is not idea-driven, is not meditative or associative or tangential."

The result, Madden suggests, is that "people don't want to read essays. Or they think they don't." But if they understood what the form really is, or should be, maybe they'd change their minds. Drawing from a few modern essayists who helped popularize the form, he invokes Samuel Johnson's "loose sally of the mind," Montaigne's "thorny undertaking … to follow a movement so wandering as that of our mind," and Virginia Woolf's "most common actions … enhanced and lit up by the association of the mind" to give us a vision of what the form should strive towards. If that's what we mean by an essay, he says, "Then count me in!"

Count *me* in, too, because in many ways this "modern" form of writing rings truer today than in Montaigne's time. Author Cheryl Strayed claimed in a 2014 *New York Times* Bookends article, "the personal essay is king"; the Internet had made it possible for essayists to attract attention simply by "many people posting a link preceded by a sentiment along the lines of *You have to read this*."

Two and a half years later, when *The New Yorker* declared the personal essay boom over, author Jia Tolentino was referring more to the first-person "TMI" essays that filled the Internet in the decade leading up to 2015. These "solo acts of sensational disclosure" that read like "reverse-engineered headlines" had become so ubiquitous that *Slate*'s Laura Bennett referred to them as a "first-person industrial complex." Of course the bubble had to burst. And though many magazines and sites are no longer publishing what Tolentino called "the ultra-confessional essay, written by a person you've never heard of," the essay lives on. In 2017, Rebecca Solnit declared a "golden age" for essays and said they're "powerful and compelling again."

Which means that for those of us who still want to write "as a person," the time is now.

We just need to remember that the essay can comprise far more than the simple school trick that goes something like "an essay is five paragraphs and a thesis statement." Does this mean the form has to be complicated? Not at all.

The essay, it turns out, is for you, even if you like the word

"I" as much as any other word in the English language and want to use it boldly—or, if you sometimes start writing before you know what you want to say and discover something new by the time you've finished. The essay is your words and your mind, lit up.

Are you ready for that? Then let's begin with an introduction.

Writer, meet the essay.

1

Listen to the Whispers

While working at my desk one summer day, I noticed my cat pawing at something on the back patio. Over the years, Kiki has practiced the unseemly habit of catching chipmunks, mice, and baby rabbits, then playing with them until they die. She leaves her toys at the back door as gifts for us. Our job is biohazard cleanup.

This time, Kiki was playing with a tiny hummingbird, the one I had invited into the yard with a glass feeder filled with red sugar water. *I should help!* Wanting to give the bird some final dignity, I went outside and firmly tapped Kiki's head. The bird dropped and began to move. Wings flapping, body wiggling, the little hummer wasn't going down without a fight.

After I engaged in a scuffle with the cat—and then the dog (who had to get in on the act)—I watched as the bird fluttered and fell, fluttered and fell, landing in a clump of hostas. The cat and the dog now safely contained, I stayed outside to see what would happen, but the foliage hid the bird's iridescent green, so I eventually went back to work. A few days later, the little bird's body had disappeared from beneath the hostas. I preserved the hummer's saga in a story on my blog.

In my life as an essayist, everything can matter. The goal, as writer Henry James famously said, is "to be one of the people on whom nothing is lost." Living with an awareness of the world creates a structure for writing that's sturdier and more beautiful than pulling from abstract ideas alone. Before

I ever introduce a topic to my audience, I meet it in real life.

Consider the hummingbird. What eventually became an essay about social outrage and personal overcoming started with the inquisitive act of going outside and experiencing a few unscripted moments with primal nature. Our inquisitiveness won't always be rewarded. Sometimes, getting up to track down a whisper (or a wallop, as the case may be) reveals only that the morning mail has come. And when I flip through to see that it's nothing but a flier from the local appliance store, I'll stop for a glass of water on the way back to my desk, and that will be that.

Still, all around me are the beginnings, the endings, and even the middles of my next essays. I don't want to miss them. So I live with awareness. I save the hummingbird, I track down the sounds, I follow my curiosity around the neighborhood or into the grocery store. As a writer, I start where I am.

But that's not where I end. To transform the everyday stuff of life into subjects I'll write about, I need more. I need to attend to what lives in pixels and airwaves and the pages of books. So I read, I listen, I watch … expectantly.

The day after I wrote about the hummingbird, I heard a story on WBUR's *Here and Now* about Terry Masear, who rescues and rehabilitates hummingbirds in Los Angeles. Injured hummingbirds don't just get up and fly, Masear said. They need a skilled rehabber.

I thought for days about my little bird, how unskilled I had been when I trusted the hostas to do the job of cover and rehab. I rehearsed the sequence of events. What could I have done differently? The degree to which I practically sentenced that bird to death would have changed the tone, if not the substance, of the story I crafted, had I known this information when I wrote it.

Then several days later as I worked at my desk, something outside again caught my eye. It was the hummingbird, zipping around our yard, zigzagging from feeder to flowerpot. For a few seconds the little bird hovered just in front of me. I almost cried. "It was like he was saying thank you," I texted to my husband. "What are the odds?"

Even Maeser would have been impressed that an unskilled rehabber like me had given a second chance to the tiny bird now skimming the dragon wing begonias.

This is how we listen to the whispers: we notice patterns, we make note of repetition, we look for the threads that weave together disparate bits of information. The hummingbird's plight, as I'd first understood it, made a fine metaphor for a blog post. But combined with the information from *Here and Now* and the subsequent sightings of the little bird, who is very much alive and well, the story took a different turn.

To say that nothing is wasted for me as an essayist is not to say that I notice *everything* or that I even *use* everything I notice. Rather, everything I notice is considered. Everything is weighed and synthesized against everything else. To do so, all this stuff of life, the observations and details of my days, needs to be gathered and stored for later.

Over the years, my laptop has become a digital commonplace book, like the small notebook popularized during the Renaissance, which Barbara M. Benedict describes as "one means of coping with the information overload of that era." (Information overload? Just imagine the Renaissance *plus* the Internet.) In various apps and files, I collect quotes and ideas or tap out observations and curiosities. Later, if I can remember even a word or two of what I typed, I can search for and find what I need. With a simple Internet search, or a dive into Google Books or Amazon's "Search Inside" feature, I can even find more specific quotations from magazines or books. Of course I can also rifle through a desk drawer, flip through the pages of a paperback, or scour a box of old letters and journals to find things that aren't accessible digitally. I've done that, too.

But I've also lost ideas, because I didn't take the time to type them out. I've scribbled a thought and later not remembered what it meant. On a few occasions, I've recognized that the details around me might solve a mystery or help me understand something important about my life. I know I'll want to remember this later, but I don't have a way to capture it. I *will* myself to take it all in, to keep it close, and I walk away thinking I'll never forget this feeling, this scene, this instant.

And then it's gone, like the hummingbird that disappeared beneath the hostas. The memory flits just beneath my consciousness, and I regret that I didn't do more to preserve it. Sometimes, if I'm very lucky, it shows up again, hovering right in front of me for a few seconds until, this time, I can hold on to it forever.

2

Memory & Truth

"Steve and I are thinking about buying a tent and sleeping bags and going camping with the boys some weekends this summer," I told Mom as I drove her back to her apartment. We had spent the afternoon at a cousin's baby shower.

"Hmmmm, that could be fun," she said, watching the empty fields pass by through the window. In our part of Indiana, you can see for miles, especially in the leaf-bare winter.

"We thought we'd buy just the minimum and see if we even like camping before we go all out."

"That's smart," Mom said, "'cause you didn't really like camping when you were a kid." My right eyebrow raised—always a signal that I'm confused or frustrated.

"What do you mean? I remember liking to camp. What part didn't I like?" Was this mom's stroke talking? Had she forgotten what I was like as a kid? Or had I forgotten my own life and interests?

"Well, you didn't really like being outside."

"Huh. I don't remember that at all. Like when I was little? Because when I was in high school, I used to go camping with friends and liked it. And when I was in college and just out of college, I went camping a lot."

"Yeah, you were more of an inside kid," she said simply.

"Oh, do you mean like I was little and you and Dad were outside chopping firewood or picking up sticks and I wanted to stay inside?"

"Yeah, you preferred being inside," she said. "We'd all go outside and you'd just stay in and read."

"Well, that was because I didn't like to work!" We both laughed. "I liked being outside, but I didn't like *doing work* outside. I didn't even like doing work *inside*. Remember how I would dust the TV by lying on the floor and using my feet so I could keep watching cartoons?"

We both cracked up again. I definitely remember being that kid.

"I think I liked being outside," I said, trying to convince myself more than mom. "And just look how hard I work now. Not lazy at all."

Mom just smiled.

Since last year when she moved into a senior apartment complex a couple of minutes away from us, my mother and I have spent more time together than any period since I was a child. I go to her apartment at least once a week for lunch, and another time each week to help with chores or tasks. We walk on the sidewalk around the perimeter of her building when the weather's nice, and we drive to the YMCA and use the NuStep stationary bike when it's not. I take her to doctor appointments and the grocery store, and when she doesn't want to get out, I deliver the groceries.

Mom needs me now in the ways I used to need her. And while I'm the one with the better day-to-day memory of where she stores the Scotch tape and when we need to pick up the prescriptions, Mom's long-term memory rounds out the story of my life with different childhood images than the ones I've carried into adulthood. Ultimately, our time together is transforming both of us—in the present as we navigate new roles, and in the past as we compare and reconcile memories of ourselves and of one another.

This is the work of writers, too, especially those of us who use our personal memories as a private storehouse of ideas. With memory, we're never actually recreating events or relationships or places. We're only recreating what we remember about them, and there's a big difference. At best, "what we can do," writes Bill Roorbach, in *Writing Life Stories: How to Make Memories into Memoirs*, "is listen to memory and watch memory (the other senses are involved, as well—who hasn't been transported back by a taste, a fragrance, a touch?) and translate memory for those we want to reach, our readers."

See, "memory has its own story to tell," as Tobias Wolff has written. It produces a truth that's clearer and dearer to us than facts or recordkeeping could ever achieve. Memory holds on to part of the places and people and events, and each time we dust off a memory and offer it to others, it becomes more a part of who we are.

We all know, writer and reader alike, that memory has limits. We know this even from the stories shared during a family reunion or a holiday gathering. "Remember that time when Mom … ," and our brother recounts the moment nothing like we remember it. But when we come to the page with these discrepancies, we owe it to ourselves and our readers to push in and get as close to the truth as possible. That's the rest of the Tobias Wolff quote, the part we don't hear as often: "Memory has its own story to tell. But I have done my best to make it tell a truthful story." When it comes to essay writing, there can be no other kind.

How do we do this—write our stories truthfully when memory is vague? For one, we can verify the details through letters, photographs, journals, public records, or calendars. We can also ask for clarification from others who were there. They might not remember either, or their memory might be different and equally subjective. But they can at least help us know if our memory "sounds right." When it comes to memories, that's often as close to perfect as we can get.

I can also let my narrator self wrestle with uncertain memories right on the page, what writer Lisa Knopp calls "perhapsing." Using words like "perhaps" or "may have been" or "I imagine" to cue the reader, writers can make their best guesses about what someone might have been thinking or what might have happened.

Maybe the best way to make memory tell a truthful story, though, is to spend time with the memory, digging deeper and deeper for evidence of what is true. When memory's footage looks hazy at first, that's when I pull the reels off the shelf and restore them through intensive retracing. I start by pushing into my mind for the details I *do* remember. Photos and journal entries often help. If I can recall one detail, usually others will follow. What year was it? What else would have been happening? Which house did we live in? Who was my best friend? I think, write, push deeper.

Recently, while working on a collection of personal essays, I needed to track down a few details from the summer I spent in Ogunquit, Maine, between my sophomore and junior years of college. I located the plastic tub of old journals down in the basement, and after weeding through, I found one that covered the summer of 1991, written in the large, loopy handwriting of my younger self.

As I read, none of the necessary details materialized. Instead, I encountered the loneliness and defeat of a twenty-something who had jumped into a situation that was a little over her head. I'd been more homesick than I remembered. I resented my roommate, who caused trouble among our team members. I felt relieved when my mom came for a visit. I'd gone looking for a glimpse of the world I'd been living in; instead, I got a picture of my heart that summer. That was enough to get me started.

With the image of myself more clearly in focus, my memory began to fill in the gaps. Later I pulled up Google Maps of the little town where I'd lived. Using online newspapers and travel sites, I searched for place names and dates from that summer. I located acquaintances on social media and used IMDb to recall the films I'd seen at the local theater. And, though the facts may not be exactly right, I found that summer's truthful story.

Accumulating enough facts and details is just one side of the truth-telling coin. The other: How do we decide what to leave out?

At home, my writing desk overlooks our fenced-in back-yard, where red squirrels chase each other in death-defying scampers along the top of our shadowbox privacy fence and up the bark of a giant tulip poplar. To my left, pine book-shelves stand sentry over my work. The sun warms me as I sit at my laptop sipping apple cinnamon tea, and Tilly, my black Lab, frequently lays her head in my lap hoping for a nibble of whatever I'm snacking on. She stares at me with those big brown eyes, tail wagging expectantly.

"Okay," I tell her, and she uses her tiny front teeth to wriggle the peanuts or baby carrots from between my fingers. However many I give her, she wants more. Eventually I ignore her long enough that she lies down behind me. I know without looking because I hear the thud of her body and the clank of her collar on the floor, followed by her loud, predictable sigh. She doesn't even bother walking to her bed in front of the fireplace. I have about five minutes before she'll be back.

This is where I work. But does it bother you to know that I've left a few things out? Yes, I love the coziness of the fireplace and built-in bookshelves, though I rarely mention how dark and drafty my office feels. The sunlight that floats in and settles on my desk usually lifts my spirit, if it's not blinding me from beneath the shades. And most of the time, stopping mid-sentence to pet Tilly's belly or open the back door for her so she can chase the squirrels does provide a much-needed break. Other times, I huff at her and tell her to stop bugging me.

I could go on.

But will going to great lengths to inventory the furniture and catalog the weather resolve anything? Every time a writer sits down to compose, she will include parts of the setting and the story and exclude others. The things emphasized and the things disguised contribute to the greater good of what's written. The author, who judges and evaluates and makes those decisions, must hope that in the end readers will understand.

Of course, the path from fact to truth contains all kinds of stopping-off points for writers. Is making something up worse than omitting something that *did* happen? Does consolidating days or combining characters amount to fabrication? Does it matter if the misrepresentation was intentional? And could this whole issue be resolved by just admitting that we all do it sometimes?

Then again, every literary artifact is imbued with a little illusion, limited by the singular perspective of the writer and the memories she can recall. We write into existence the world we need, to explain the truth we believe. Like Emily Dickinson's "Tell all the truth but tell it slant," we know that writing all that's real might blind our readers or bore them or make them unpleasantly squeamish—just as we know that memory's version of events might leave out a fact or change a date or fail to provide every detail we need.

When it comes to what we write, especially what we call *nonfiction*, the standard is set high: to search for the truth. And when I'm not exactly sure what that constitutes (and this will be our little secret, okay?), I just ask my mom.

3

May I Ask?

"That doesn't look good," I said, pointing east. My husband Steve and I were driving up Indiana Highway 29 heading towards Logansport.

"What?"

"That van, out in the middle of nowhere. That doesn't look good."

Steve glanced at the maroon van. "Maybe he's just hunting."

"Hunting what? I don't think it's hunting season for *anything*."

"Maybe he's hunting mushrooms?"

"Way too early." Winter was having trouble saying goodbye that spring.

"Maybe he's checking the soil?" Steve smirked. I looked at him through narrowed eyes, then back at the field.

"I watch too many crime shows. I've concocted a far more nefarious reason for that van to be in the field," I confessed, imagining a body in the back. "I'm sure you're right. Probably just hunting or maybe checking his traps. Is it trapping season?"

Steve shrugged, and we changed the subject. But my mind didn't really let it go. Had the van still been there when we drove back by hours later, I might have insisted we stop.

I do watch an unhealthy amount of crime, spy, and mystery shows, but I don't think that's the reason I have such an inquiring mind. In fact, I think it's the other way around. I think my curiosity draws me to where I constantly wonder how the plot will turn out. I think it's also what draws me to essays.

This inquisitiveness not only leads me to the back porch to find a captured hummingbird, but it also steers me to the library, the interviewee, the magazine article, the neighborhood where I used to live. I go with some slice of evidence or a question I can't stop asking. I go looking for one answer, but I'm open to whatever I find. I read, listen, and write my way to discovery.

Dani Shapiro calls this kind of writing *inquiry*. "My novels all begin with questions—though these questions may not be ones I can articulate when I begin," she says. Shapiro came to understand the importance of the term *inquiry* when she struggled to answer, "What are you working on?" She didn't know how to describe these projects. Lyric essay? Creative nonfiction? Memoir? So she named the intent, not the form. She writes to discover what she doesn't yet know, to "peel back the layers and see what has been previously hidden from view."

Often, our thoughts, opinions, and emotions are hidden when we begin. They surface as we write, our minds themselves serving as the subject of our inquiry. We investigate, ripple outward. Eventually, we begin to think differently about essay writing. "Too often students think of the essay as a vehicle for delivering chunks of information or prefabricated ideas," writes Scott Russell Sanders, who helps students get started with writing personal essays by offering them "puzzles, questions, confusions." He believes essays require risks.

They beg us "to venture out from familiar territory into the blank places on their maps."

Author Laura Hillenbrand knows the magic of finding something unexpected, even when the journey is necessarily figurative. Plagued with chronic fatigue syndrome, she researches her highly-detailed nonfiction books by bringing source materials, even physical artifacts, into her home. Vintage newspapers, purchased on eBay, become cover-to-cover reading material, as if delivered to her door that morning.

Hillenbrand talks about a 1936 issue of *The New York Times* she read while researching her best-selling book *Seabiscuit*. "There was so much to find. The number one book was *Gone With the Wind*, the Hindenburg flew over Manhattan with a swastika on it and Roosevelt made a speech saying America would never become involved in foreign wars."

Several issues later, Hillenbrand landed on an idea for her next book. "I happened to turn over a clipping about Seabiscuit," she said. "On the other side of that page, directly the opposite side of the page, was an article on Louis Zamperini, this running phenom." Zamperini was the subject of Hillenbrand's next bestseller, *Unbroken*.

I've made a few unanticipated discoveries in my own writing investigations. Years ago, as I was researching body modification for an article about embodiment, I expected to find information about cosmetic surgery, prosthetic limbs and transplants, even tattoos and piercings. But what I didn't know to look for was an article about researchers who are trying to improve the design of the human body. Instead of just replacing limbs lost through injury or illness, they're attempting to create better functioning arms and legs. The result is a new class of cyborgs, part human and part machine. This created an important tension in my writing that I hadn't expected.

Similarly, when I wrote about an Indiana farm owned by one family for four generations, the story caught the attention of a publisher not only because the farm had been in the family for nearly two centuries, but also because it was one of the first farms purchased in Indiana by a former slave. I came to the interview with the current owner wondering how his great-great-grandfather had secured his freedom before coming to Indiana. But what I discovered was that he hadn't. As a young man, he'd been brought to our state, then part of the Northwest Territory, as a slave, and though slavery was technically outlawed in the Territory and in Indiana after statehood, a legal loophole kept him from being free until the 1820s, years after Indiana joined the Union. The lawsuit that led to this one man's freedom also brought liberty to every person who was enslaved or indentured in the county where he lived. The essay I wrote took a much different course with this information in hand.

Most of us will do at least some research on the Internet. I rely on quick Google searches to turn up facts, people, places, and more. Many essays, articles, poems, novels, memoirs, and public records are available as full-text documents.

But just as the Internet can be one of my best research tools, it can also become my worst. Even in this vast array of source materials I may not be able to find what I'm looking for; after all, Google's algorithms give preference to paid ads and sites with high-volume traffic, which might push the perfect article so far down I'll never see it. And I can't smell, taste, or touch the objects I find there. Even the sights and sounds

I uncover are limited by the span of the camera angle or the range of the microphone. When I use the Internet alone for my research, I'll miss the musty smell of the courthouse while I review the plat records of my growing-up neighborhood and I'll miss talking to a passerby who just witnessed the accident outside the restaurant where I was eating. And, of course, many older, lesser known, or obscure documents don't live on the Internet at all.

So, I use the Internet as a place to start, but I don't limit myself to it. Instead, I try to understand what sources are needed in which situations. I attempt to identify my own gate-keepers and curators, people or organizations I can trust for intriguing details. Then I visit their in-person locations or speak directly with them.

At some point, I start to feel as if I've researched enough, but I'm tempted to look for one more fact, one more quote, or one more anecdote to complete my essay. It's not so much that I need that one more thing. Instead, my research is in disarray, the ideas I started with have gotten away from me, and now I'm putting off the writing because I don't know where to start. Sound familiar?

When my investigation becomes an excuse not to write, I set it aside and begin the work of synthesizing and organizing what I've collected. Because the blank page is daunting, I follow what I call a *find 'n' fill* method. I open up a new file and type in bits of my research: quotes, key points, and stories I know I'll want to include. I don't try to put it in order or make sense of it at the beginning. Slowly, as the page begins to fill, an energy emerges, from which a direction can start to take shape.

Later, I might discover a gap in my research and head back out to investigate further—but only if it serves the writing. Otherwise, my investigations turn into cold trails instead of vital essays that take me to undiscovered territories.

4

Making Maps

A few summers ago, I regularly drove fifty-two miles round trip to a co-working studio in Lafayette, Indiana. The only thing that nearly kept me from it was the drive. Between summer construction and an old bridge that had sunk nine inches, there was no easy way to get to my destination. The route I knew best happened to be the most direct path, but the sunken bridge sits just north of the exit I'd take, and the detour shut down traffic before I could even merge onto the interstate, so I researched alternate routes.

I have always loved maps. When I was younger, my brother and I mapped an imaginary town in the briar patch in the woods behind our house. We knew just where to turn to find the large open space I claimed as my "house," and we followed the main "road" to the right and around to the sections my brother claimed. When our family moved to the other end of town just before my second-grade year, our new six-acre plot offered us a blank slate. We built trails for the mini-bike and the lawn mower and drove them repeatedly. On foot, we mapped out an alternate path that took us from our back porch, along the mini-bike trail, down into the hollow, across the creek, and back up to the porch again.

When it came to skirting all the traffic and detours to get to the co-working studio, my inner child returned. Sometimes I'd open up the Maps app on my phone, zooming and panning to try to connect the lines and curves on the screen. One road I found, Ninth Street, had fewer stoplights than the rest, and another, Kossuth, took me past the most beautiful turn-of-the-century homes with large porches and sharp-edged gables crowning every roof. I tried to include those streets in any route I attempted.

Finding my way as a writer offers similar challenges. Once I've collected observations or research and formed my ideas, I begin mapping my essay. I often rely on the most direct route: the *find 'n' fill* method mentioned in the previous chapter. Then I'll look to include a personal story, and more often than not, the particular beauty of nature or art wriggle their way into my writing. Sometimes a turn in my research or the sinking of what first seemed like a good idea will force me to abandon my process and try a new route. Occasionally, I'll be cruising along when a turn of phrase on the radio will be the best whim I could follow as I map out where to go with my words. Once I get three items with a common thread, I know I'm onto something good. The essay doesn't have to be mapped out completely to start writing. As Scott Russell Sanders explains it, we just need a "critical mass of ideas, images, memories, speculations, and associations" before we begin. If we are feeling stuck, it's quite likely we just don't have that critical mass yet.

In my educational experience beginning around grade 9, I was required to have my conclusion made and written on a 3-by-5 index card, along with each shred of evidence I planned to present to support three main points that would prove the conclusion, before I ever began writing the essay. During my formative years, that method pushed me to think logically, support my claims, and give others credit when I borrowed their words or original ideas. These skills seem more necessary than ever as we wrestle with confirmation bias, "alternative facts," and fake news.

What the academic essay *didn't* teach me was how to play with ideas, how to not only support them but refute them, and how to use my "self," the me I could pluck from real life and recreate on paper like Montaigne did, to engage readers. After learning the academic essay in high school, I entered college as a mass communications major and learned the equally formulaic news article approach with its inverted pyramid structure that front loads the important bits of the story at the top, its Associated Press style, and its dogged commitment to let the story stand with no editorializing. I learned to chase down stories, ask good questions, and quickly identify what was most important for the lead. Like the academic essay, though, journalism didn't let me play and question and get personally wrapped up in the ideas.

The grade 9 notecard approach and the inverted pyramid approach ask us to come to the page almost as if we'd already written the essay in our heads and are simply about to commit our invisible essay to print, while my own current strategy of choice is often to just start writing, after a season of *find 'n' fill*. But is there a middle ground, where a writer can see at a glance, map-style, whether they have critical mass (while also strengthening associations, breaking and remaking them)— before going too far?

Mind mapping offers one strategy for following whims and connecting the dots before committing any significant acts of prose. Mind maps start with an idea scribbled inside a circle in the middle of the page. Then, they grow as we expand each idea by writing down associated words and topics. Each new entry is drawn with a line from the original circle and then circled itself. The words in each new circle offer more opportunity to dive deeper into the topic, with new sets of lines and new circled words.

Below, for instance, is a mind map I created about the topic of *adumbration*, which is a writing technique used to intimate deeper meaning or build tension, through the passing inclusion of repeated and related objects or places over the course of an article or book.

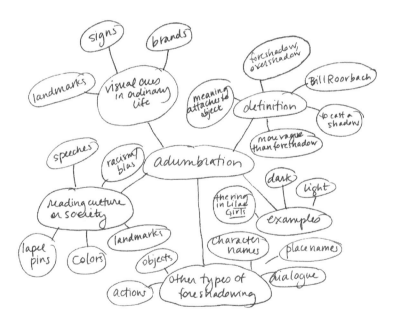

Unlike basic brainstorming, where every idea exists equally on one big list, mind mapping nests related ideas and allows you to drill down into each area while still seeing the relationships between them. Mind maps also produce something like an outline, but they aren't nearly as formal. In fact, in a single mind map, you might end up with one or two developed essay ideas, and the beginning of several more.

While I've mainly used analog mind maps—the kind you draw on actual paper using a pen or pencil—you can also use digital tools such as LiquidText or MindNode to generate them. In the same way word processing apps allow you to easily correct errors or rearrange paragraphs, digital mind mapping tools allow you to move ideas and connect them in ways that weren't initially apparent, without having to start over on a new sheet of paper (or burn through an eraser if you try to correct as you go). Additionally, an app like LiquidText has the added benefit of tracking sources for you, if you are mapping partly by dropping in snippets of articles. This is helpful not only for bibliography time, but also for when you write your essay and might want to reread the original context of your snippet or find additional quotes.

Another way to map your essay involves those same notecards from my high school days—but with a twist. While each notecard from my ninth grade research paper included the corresponding number to my outline, ideas can remain much more fluid in the "train of thought" method.

Start by jotting down your main ideas and supporting anecdotes on the notecards, then lay them on a table or even across the floor in the order that seems right. But before committing to the order, try rearranging the cards. What if the anecdote you were planning to end with actually served as your introduction? How would your argument build if you reversed the order of your main points? Now that you see your train of thought lying in front of you, is there a gap in your structure? With this method, you can arrange and rearrange over and over until you feel like you're ready to write.

Incidentally, this same method might be just the thing you need when you're ready to revise your essay later in the process. In this case, you might skip the notecards and simply print out your manuscript and cut it apart paragraph by paragraph. Then, play around with the structure before committing to changes in your actual manuscript.

That summer I drove to the coworking studio, the highway stayed closed for months, but after a few weeks I hardly even noticed. By then, I preferred the new routes I'd mapped, with its pleasing views of porches and gables. The same thing happens when we take the time to map our essays. We start with the most obvious paths, the ones we've taken before in our writing. But we don't stop there. We run a finger over our lines of reasoning, looking for a different course. We make unexpected connections between our ideas and anecdotes. We try out a different road than the one we set out upon. And, in the end, we often like the views even better.

5

Show, Tell, Explain

When I was in kindergarten, my teacher practiced the time-honored tradition of show and tell. Each week, a different student brought a treasured item to present to the class. Of course the most valued possessions of five- and six-year-olds often include an assortment of, by adult standards, decidedly valueless items. Mrs. Flora didn't seem to mind.

For my turn, I brought "Oof Oof," a stuffed yellow dog who was my version of Linus' dusty blue blanket. I took him everywhere I was allowed and refused to go to sleep without him by my side. Oof Oof had been a gift from my Aunt Pat when I was born, and by the time I was old enough to talk, I called him Oof Oof after my Grandma Ruth.

Fast-forward to kindergarten, and Oof Oof's appearance no longer matched his exalted status in my life. His yellow fur was matted and greyed, his eyelashes had been partly ripped off, and his shape had gone from firm and defined to rather soft and lumpy. I don't remember the response as I stood holding Oof Oof in front of the classroom, my classmates watching from their swivel chairs attached to metal desks, but I do know that since he wasn't much to look at, I did far more telling than showing that day. Appearances could be deceiving.

Appearances can also be deceiving in our writing, which is why, despite the oft-quoted advice to "show, not tell," *telling* has far more purpose in our stories and especially our essays than it's given credit for. I like the metaphor Gail Carson Levine uses in her book *Writing Magic*. She says *telling* is like being in an airplane and describing what you see below; "only the biggest landmarks stand out." *Showing*, she says, is like being on the ground; we can see all the details. "What you want is a writer's telescope, so you can increase or decrease the magnification: increase to show, decrease to tell."

I think about the advice to "show, not tell" more along the lines of "tell only what you can't show," since so much of our writing is actually *telling*. When you rephrase the advice, it still holds up against a line attributed to Anton Chekhov: "Don't tell me the moon is shining; show me the glint of light on broken glass." That's a moon I'd like to see. It also works with Mark Twain's famous "Don't say, 'The old lady screamed.' Bring her on and let her scream." In fact, I can hear her now. It hurts my ears just thinking about it. But what about Ernest Hemingway's "Show the readers everything, tell them nothing"? Of all the writers in the world, he comes about as close as any to actually following that advice. Still, he often wrote about things that had meaning beyond what was immediately apparent, especially in nonfiction work like *A Moveable Feast*. In that case, he spent at least some of the time explaining the things that had happened in his life.

So, what's the real difference between *showing* and *telling* in our essays? *Showing* is all about the observable action, dialogue, and basic details of the story. It's delivered in real time and set up like scenes in a movie. *Telling*, on the other hand, is the work of a narrator to summarize, condense, and describe. It gives us context, backstory, and ideas. Together, the two form stories, where scenes often reveal the most important information, but they're connected by narrative summary. S*howing* and *telling* work in concert.

In essays, there's another dimension to *telling*, one that requires a third category to contain it. That category is *exposition*, or *explaining*. *Exposition* operates in the dimension of abstract ideas, examining and analyzing information and events. It draws from facts, opinions, cultural observations, and personal experiences. In fact, explaining often sets essays apart from other types of creative nonfiction, like memoir, travel writing, or journalism. It's the X factor that allows for exploration, inquiry, and even counterpoint to the life circumstances, the destination, or the story being written. It's the way most of this book has been written.

Showing, *telling*, and *explaining* work in conjunction to create writing that is both concrete and abstract. I've never found a magic formula for combining these three elements, and I don't suggest spending a lot of time parsing out when we're doing which. In fact, in *The Making of a Story*, Alice LaPlante says it's often very difficult to "clinically dissect all showing and telling" (and I'll add *explaining*). Instead, we can reach for making the three work together—to create scenes that enliven the reader's experience, narrative summary that occasionally speeds things along, and exposition that helps reveal why it's important.

When a professor or peer reviewer suggests that the author "show, not tell," it's often because of a lack of balance among the three. Sometimes the balance is off as a result of poor *telling*, "because good telling is difficult to do," LaPlante notes. Other times, the writer is being too abstract when more concrete details are available and would make the story come alive. But the problem rarely will be resolved by more *showing* alone, as the advice would suggest.

Think of it like this: Today as I write, I'm sitting on a leather loveseat in front of a large gas fireplace in the plank-floored lounge of Turkey Run State Park. A few minutes ago, I took a walk outside, where the sun warmed my shoulders and face but the cool breeze reminded me it's only March. Still, 48 degrees isn't bad, and I walked around comfortably, for a few minutes at least, in black leggings, a T-shirt, and a plaid flannel tunic.

I can show you the black mallard I saw earlier, honking wildly as he floated down muddy Sugar Creek. I can show you the sun, refracted brightly through the windows, and the wind, dancing a tango with the Indiana and U.S. flags hanging proudly in front of the inn where I'm staying. I can show you the bare limbs of the trees slithering into the blue expanse of the sky. And showing you these things is enough to bring you here with me for a moment, *this* moment.

But this present scene reveals nothing of the storms moving west and south out of the Rockies and Canada that will bring rain and snow for the weekend. The Weather Channel reveals that information, while research with the National Weather Service might explain what's causing the warmer than average temperatures and the impending unseasonably harsh winter storm—and how this might contribute to an overall understanding of climate.

This is how scenes, narrative summary, and exposition work together. Some elements can be felt and seen, like the wind whipping my hair around my face. We can offer them to readers in near real time, inviting them to experience the scene with us. But other things have to be described and summarized in order to bring the reader up to speed (or to speed the text along), like the weather patterns not immediately obvious. Still others have to be explained—analyzed and interpreted—to help the reader understand, or at least recognize, the questions we're asking. Things like climate breakdown and more.

Using all three methods is as elementary as it is complex; a careful combination will help the reader value your words.

6

Place It

One year, I celebrated Earth Day in a hospital waiting room. My plans to commemorate the occasion, by spending intentional time around the little patch of earth I call home, were delayed. Instead, I sat vigil with a friend whose husband was fighting for his life in the ICU. We talked quietly in the waiting room and wept bitterly over the unfairness that had descended so suddenly on their lives.

Later that evening, hoping to redeem the last bits of daylight, I headed outside to pick up trash along the country roads of my neighborhood. Collecting cans and bottles, paper bags and Styrofoam seemed like such a small way to try to save the planet. All I was doing was tending a strip of ground between the tilled fields and the paved road—a slim grass section that collects runoff rain in summer and plowed snow in winter and might occasionally attract a bird or a mouse. It's not even large enough to host a deer or fox.

With each bit of rubbish I gathered, I thought of my friend fighting for his life. I thought of the warm touches and the tight hugs and the weeping and praying we did together in the waiting room outside the intensive care unit, and I understood that very small acts are sometimes the only way we can show our care.

I walked back to the smell of freshly cut grass and wild flowers. When I got home, I stuffed the large bag of trash I'd gathered into the plastic bin, to be picked up on our usual garbage day. As I closed the lid, I realized that these bits of plastic and glass and paper no longer littering our neighborhood will instead end up in the landfill just a few miles from our house.

The next day, I was still thinking about the earth as I dropped off our recyclables at the local street department barn. I was glad that, because we took time to rinse and deliver them, none of these things would be in the landfill.

As is often the case, Robert was there. The spry elderly man, who has worked for our city's street department for decades, seems to run the recycling barn.

"Do you know what the IDEM is?" he asked me as he carried a scoop over to the plastics receptacle.

"Did you say 'IDEM' – I-D-E-M?" I clarified.

"Yes, IDEM," he repeated.

"Indiana Department of Environmental Management?"

"That's right. They're coming for an inspection this week," he told me, leaning in close like it was a secret. "The place has to be spotless … inside." So, in addition to emptying the receptacles, he was ordering the trucks out of the building and scrubbing away the oil leaks with dishwashing detergent.

"I'm so glad you guys do such a good job with recycling," I told him. "Every time I drive past the big dump, I think about how important it is to recycle." I pointed northwest, as if he didn't know about the big dump.

Then he told me about the mayor who decided in 1988 that our city needed a recycling program. He mentioned the trip he took with other street department employees to observe the LaPorte, Ind., recycling program. Then he told me how he and the other employees built this recycling barn with their own hands.

Their own hands.

It's the hands that made Earth Day special for me that year. Hands holding, tending, collecting, bringing healing to my friend and to the margin areas.

And it's the hands, and details like them—placed in a vibrant context—that bring our essays to life. An ordinary Earth Day cleanup is made palpable through the smell of fresh-cut grass with the sight of cornflowers by the side of an Indiana highway. The sound of an old man's voice, whispering secrets, helps our readers move within our words and ideas.

Some details are easier to come by than others. Out of the five senses we rely on for details—seeing, hearing, touching, tasting, and smelling—visual descriptions are the most common. The flax-colored Roman shades in my office, the dark oak trim around the windows, the emerald grass: we jump to *seeing* first as we show our readers what's before us. But a sight-based approach might reflect more of a 21st-century Western preference than a universally appealing story craft or aesthetic taste. In analyzing multiethnic writing, author and editor Namrata Poddar concluded that non-Western writers rely on the sense of hearing more, "play[ing] persistently with language, sounds and syntax." So I switch my attention, and there it is: the *sh-sh-sh* of the maple trees, the hum of the space heater running next to me, the soft *coo-oo* of the mourning doves. And why stop there? I switch my attention again and detect the fragrance of the Honeycrisp apple candle sitting on the Hoosier cabinet behind me.

Maybe that's enough? I could also tell you about the acidic

tomato juice I had today—two tiny cans, actually—but how does that fit into the story? Or, does it matter that the finish on the floor beneath my office chair has worn away and now the wood is so smooth it's almost slippery when I move the chair?

Without describing what's around us, we'll tell readers what we could have shown them, and their experience of our context will be muted. But if our descriptions are slowing the pace, irrelevant to the action, or excessive beyond what anyone would likely notice, then they need to be scaled back. How do we know when we've included enough description? Or too much?

Wendell Berry says we provide the right amount of detail about the places we're writing by imagining the questions readers will ask. "No human work can become whole by including everything," he writes in *Imagination in Place*, "but it can become whole in another way: by accepting its formal limits and then answering within those limits all the questions it raises." Our work, then, is to anticipate the questions readers will have and answer with just enough detail that they can fill in the rest.

At the very least, this means writing from a familiar knowledge of the places we're describing. For instance, Berry says if a farmer is a writer, he'll "at least call farming tools and creatures by their right names, will be right about the details of work, and may extend the same courtesy to other subjects." We also need to "get sophisticated about carnal writing," as Mary Karr describes in *The Art of Memoir*. Our goal is not to inundate the reader with random specifics but to "select sensual data—items, odors, sounds—to recount details based on their psychological effects on a reader." We need our descriptions to mean something; we need our places to be significant.

Sometimes, in order to find this balance—answering questions a place might raise without filling in too many of the blanks—we may need to get away from a place, to see it from afar as our readers would. Sometimes, we need to write from a different place.

When Annie Dillard was writing *Pilgrim at Tinker Creek*, she spent much of her time perched in a study carrel in the Hollins University library. "Writers very often need to be away from a place to write about it well," Dillard explained in an interview. Henrik Ibsen was living in Italy when he wrote about his beloved Norway. Willa Cather's novels of life on the prairie were drafted in New York City. James Joyce wrote his Dublin works while in Paris. Mark Twain lived in Hartford, Connecticut, when he wrote his famous stories of life on the Mississippi. "That's called critical distance or something," Dillard said. "You have to have it."

Critical distance helps the places of my past become whole again in my mind. When I'm away, the questions I must answer become obvious because I'm asking them myself. Maybe the critical distance also helps *me* feel whole, so I can go back to a place and become part of it again. That's the challenge in our writing, says Scott Russell Sanders, to both engage with and separate from the subjects we write about and the people we're surrounded by. On the one hand, you have to "be faithful at once to your vision and your place, to the truth you have laboriously found and the people whom this truth might serve." On the other, simply getting the work done often means "I must withdraw into solitude, must close my door against the world and close my mind against the day's news." If I strike the balance, the writing will usher me back "to the life of family, friends, and neighbors with renewed energy and insight."

If not, Sanders says, "Then it has failed."

So we start where we are, in the places we currently inhabit. We also push into the past, to the places we've been. But always, we reach for the hands. Because it's the hands that make the writing, and the writing life, so good.

7

Write Them In

My younger brother and I were engrossed in a conversation about reading and thinking, when we were interrupted by an invitation to say grace. We'd been rehearsing for my sister's wedding, and now we were spread across the banquet room of the local National Guard Armory.

I bowed my head, sitting next to my brother, who didn't pray much at the time.

As the minister neared the "Amen," he said, "Thank you, God, for these friends we are gathered with." I felt myself nodding in agreement, until I realized that not one person there was my friend. They were all family, or future family. And for that kind of folks—kinfolks—the minister offered no such thanks.

When grace ended and we all looked up, I stared straight at my brother.

"Do you think we'd be friends if we weren't related?" I asked, dead serious.

"Probably not," he said, meaning it.

"You're probably right. You'd think I was a prude."

"And you'd think I was a jackass."

We both laughed.

"But we might," I decided, wanting to defend the relationship we've worked hard on over the years. At the time, he was an agnostic who drank beer on the weekends and told crude jokes, and I was (and still am) a Christian who drinks lattes and attends bible studies. We've worked hard to stay close, be open-minded, know when to just be quiet.

Over the years, our differing opinions have become more closely aligned, each of us gravitating a little more to the center. We often talk about labor law and immigration, big business and our environment. We swap work stories about office politics and corporate headaches. And we really love talking about his two sons and his beautiful wife.

"We're family. But we'd also probably be friends."

Nick agreed. "Yeah, I think you're right, Sis." He leaned back in his metal folding chair. "I think we would be friends."

"But where would we hang out?" I asked, laughing.

"Good question."

A few weeks after that conversation, I wrote an essay about it on my blog. My brother and I had been together again, this time to celebrate birthdays, and thinking back on that conversation at the armory, I had bought him a subscription to a current events magazine as a gift. It was the occasion of the gift that pushed me towards writing.

Did I check with my brother first before hitting publish on that post? No, though I did get his permission to include the story here now. His response to the initial publication of the story was delivered just as publicly as the post, which came to his attention via social media.

"I feel famous now. I love you so much!" he wrote on Facebook. "You're not only my big sister and hero but one of my best friends and I am so lucky we met, family or not."

The opportunity to explore family ties in the context of stark differences, especially when the two of us actually get along so well, seemed hard to pass up. Did I know that's how it was going to work out when I published the piece without my brother's permission? Especially one that so specifically characterizes him spiritually, politically, and relationally? No. Not really. But my relationship with him suggested he'd take it well, especially since the details I "revealed" were actually things many people already know about him. I was glad it worked out.

Interestingly, not only did my brother not cry foul for my public recounting of a private conversation, but my baby sister was "offended" I'd left her out.

"Come on, Sis, I was sitting at the table too at this exact moment and you don't mention me?" she said in another Facebook comment. "What the heck? Now Nick is rubbing it in my face that he has a blog [post about him] and I don't. When I move in with you I better be blogged! Love you!"

So, as any good writer would, I took this invitation as carte blanche to write about my sister during the three months she lived with me while completing an internship. And just as I suspected, she was delighted I did.

Of course there are things I'll never write about my family, events too personal or embarrassing or painful to bring to light at all. Ever. When my stepdad died almost six years ago, I wrote a eulogy for his funeral. Since then I've barely mentioned him in anything else I've written. I want to. He left such a deep impression on my life. Brief stories of our mutual lives have begun to show up in a few personal essays I've written. This man raised me, for goodness' sake. How can I write about my past and not mention him? For that matter, how can I even write about my present and not mention him? His influence—and his love—lingers in my life. But the story of my grief and the process of carrying on without him can't be told without creating greater pain for others. So I don't write much about him. Not yet.

In an interview for *Quotidiana*, Scott Russell Sanders talks about writing his essay "Under the Influence," an account of his father's alcoholism and death from the disease. When he first wrote it, he showed it to his mother. She was so hurt by it that she begged Sanders not to publish it. So he didn't. Later, his siblings heard about his hidden draft.

"They found the essay so helpful in dealing with their own troubled memories that they prevailed on my mother to let me publish it, so that other readers might be helped," he recounted. Once his mother gave her blessing, the essay was published in *Harper's* magazine and reprinted in anthologies more than forty times. But had his mother not consented, he said he'd "have left the essay in my drawer, at least so long as she was alive."

We each have to draw our own line between what we will share and what we won't. It's a critical aspect of writing about others. "How much can we show of our families' private lives before we become crude carnival hawkers, selling out their oddities and crimes—See the bearded lady!—for our own art?" writes Joy Castro.

One way to handle this dilemma is to wait until the time feels more right. I've seen many interviews with memoirists who are writing now because a family member has died, a relationship is healed, or a marriage has ended.

Of course not everyone agrees with the idea of waiting. A few years ago, author Anne Lamott humorously tweeted,

"You own everything that happened to you. Tell your stories. If people wanted you to write warmly about them, they should've behaved better." If you are not concerned about your friends' and family's responses when you write about them or if you feel the good of sharing your story outweighs the pain your words may bring them, then Lamott's conclusion may be yours, too. It's also how memoirist Sue William Silverman thinks. "As scary as possible judgment or rejection might be, remember: You can't control anyone's reactions. All you can do is write your truths, refuse to continue living in silence, or living a lie," she says.

At the same time, writing stories that include others might bring us closer to our friends and family, as my writing about my brother did. Silverman also highlights a *Fourth Genre* interview with author Kim Barnes, who suggests writers shouldn't assume that the people in their lives will be angered if they're written about. "If you … treat people … with complexity and compassion, sometimes they will feel as though they've been honored," she said, "not because they're presented in some ideal way but because they're presented with understanding."

That word, *understanding*, may offer the best guidance for how we share stories about others. Do we resist the stereotypes and caricatures often utilized in melodrama and situational comedies? Do we write about our people like Wendell Berry's farmer I mentioned in the last chapter, with an intimate knowledge of where they come from? Have we taken the time to really know the people in our lives who have become characters in our writing? Do we connect with our friends and family in our writing?

In an interview about her memoir *The Faraway Nearby*,

Rebecca Solnit discusses the process of writing about her brush with cancer while also writing about her mother's Alzheimer's disease. She hadn't realized all the connections between the two events until she began writing. "When I write I find out things—sometimes quite compromising things—about myself I might not have otherwise," Solnit explains. She also found that juxtaposing these two instances of suffering provided a way to more fully connect with her mother, from whom she'd otherwise been estranged. Through writing she was reminded "that we don't know ourselves perfectly, let alone others; we're just explorers."

For years, I've teased my family that what they do is fodder for my writing. "Watch out," I've heard my mom say to anyone doing anything slightly embarrassing, "she'll put that in her book." That was even before I was married, before I lived with a husband and three stepsons whose lives are like idea factories for me, who are always saying and doing things that would make great essays. Occasionally, I grab an idea and run with it. But often, I ask before writing about them. I have to live with these people, after all.

Not all our friends and family members might feel the same about being included in an essay or memoir, even with their permission. One way around this dilemma is to change the identifying characteristics of a person or combine multiple people into one. In *Writing Life Stories*, Bill Roorbach not only offers strategies for doing so, he models it through his own characters who appear in multiple chapters. He also demonstrates the importance of telling the reader what you are doing, as a way to honor the pact that nonfiction writers have with readers to tell the truth.

Some characters cannot be masked, however—I have only one husband, for instance (and that works for me!). Plus, not all characters lend themselves to composites—some quirks are so unique and obvious that they can't be buried within the life of someone else.

I once heard author Lauren Winner address this question of writing about others in a Q&A session at a conference. An audience member asked how she decides what to write and what to leave out. At that time, Winner had just published her memoir *Girl Meets God*, so it was an issue she'd recently faced. She talked about how she made those decisions, but then she suggested that if an author doesn't feel free to write a story fully, then maybe the story isn't ready to be told.

It was a bracing moment for everyone in the room, as if Winner had just sucked the life out of our writing dreams. But it also was liberating. Because when the time is right—when we've gotten permission or we don't think we need permission—the story of our relationship with others becomes a bridge we cross over towards greater healing or deeper relationship, or sometimes simply to better understand ourselves.

8

I'm Speaking: First-Person Voice

I knew I wanted to be a journalist years before I worked in the *Banner Graphic* newsroom in Greencastle, Indiana. From the second-floor desk where I sat, I could look down on Jackson Street and out towards Franklin and across to the courthouse where I often attended meetings of the county commissioners and the zoning and planning board. I could walk out of the building, turn west on Franklin, pass the hardware store, and head down Market Street to land at the county jail and the sheriff's department and collect the daily citation and arrest reports.

Though I could also walk to the courthouse, most of the meetings were in the evenings. So I would drive back to the office in my little red Chevette, park next to the *Banner Graphic*, and run across the street with a bag full of steno pads and ballpoint pens, the newspaper's large printing presses watching over me through floor-to-ceiling windows.

For the first several months, I floated through my assignments, and at the water fountain one day, I remarked to a coworker, "I can't believe they pay me to do this." The *Banner Graphic* served up a daily afternoon paper to a small rural community. We took Sundays off; at least the team that ran the press and delivered the papers did. Some of us still covered events and wrote stories through the weekend even though they wouldn't be published until Monday. Violent storms, fatal accidents on the interstate, even the county fair and its opening parade: they didn't wait for normal business hours.

That's one reason that, after a year into the job, I began to dread it. The lack of a regular schedule made having a life outside of work nearly impossible. I also noticed that the news cycle in my small town took a strangely familiar turn as we flipped the last page of the calendar to a new year. Before long, it felt like I was sitting in the same meetings and writing the same stories that filled the boxes of yellowing newsprint stacked in our archive room.

Then there were the phone calls from sources who alternately demanded or resented coverage, depending on what they had to gain or lose. As a reporter, I had some say in what stories I covered, but not much. And the man who did have the say also had the wisdom to hold his ground. For some reason those callers didn't have his number, though.

What ultimately propelled me out of the newsroom was my inability to find myself in the stories I was writing. I would be overwhelmed by a serious incident—one time I even ran alongside the interstate in strappy sandals trying to get a crash story—yet I couldn't inject my emotions or my fear into the stories. I covered the trial of a man accused of causing shaken baby syndrome, and while I was pulled back and forth between guilty and not guilty with each new piece of evidence, my own opinion was entirely irrelevant.

Then there were the county commissioners. Over and over their discussions would go in circles because, as was apparent to me, they just didn't listen to or understand each other. Oh, how I wanted to clear my throat, lift my hand and wave it around a little, and say timidly, "Maybe I can help here." Instead, I took deep calming breaths and doodled on my steno pad as the three men tried to work things out amongst themselves.

In that way, I guess you could say I knew before I knew— I was destined to be an essayist, not a journalist. For years, I thought it was my voice that was missing, that in the quest for objectivity I couldn't offer my perspective. I now see that it wasn't just my voice or perspective that I longed to inject into those quickly crafted news stories day after day.

It was me.

But there's a problem when we try to write ourselves into our essays. "Selves, as it turns out, are awfully complicated," notes Bill Roorbach in *Writing Life Stories*, which means that bringing my self, or the first person, into my essay isn't as easy as it seems. For one, I'll never be fully myself. I'll never fit all of me into anything I write. Especially all of the me's I've been across time. The self I am now is not the self I once was or will be. Which self will I introduce to readers today? Which part of my younger self can best tell the story? Is the me of the future beckoning me to dream and hope and run towards something unexpected?

Of course how much of myself I include in the essay depends on my meaning, purpose, and audience. Is the self a narrator? Is the self a subject? Is the self simply the author who has been places and done things and now thinks differently as a result? I have to choose, because as Scott Russell Sanders says, "What we meet on the page is not the flesh-and-blood author, but a simulacrum, a character who wears the label I." Over time, though, "the self that emerges from the page again and again, in essay after essay, accumulates into a style or a voice." Eventually, your readers will begin to recognize you, hidden in the words.

According to Strunk and White, in their iconic *Elements of Style*, that's the best way to work towards developing your stylized self anyway. Rather than setting out with the goal to improve style or develop a personalized writing voice, they recommend that writers try to become "proficient in the use of language." In doing so, they say, "your style will emerge, because you yourself will emerge, and when this happens you will find it increasingly easy to break through the barriers that separate you from other minds, other hearts."

Verlyn Klinkenborg's advice sounds similarly comforting. "'Style' shouldn't linger in your awareness. You don't need to think about style," he writes in *Several Short Sentences About Writing*...

> It's as likely to appear in the character of your thinking, the shape of your ideas, your sense of humor or irony, as it is in any 'stylistic' markers in the prose itself. But this will only be true if your prose is clear enough to reveal the character of your thinking, the shape of your ideas, and your sense of humor or irony. Where ambiguity rules, there is no 'style'—or anything else worth having. Pursue clarity instead. In the pursuit of clarity, style reveals itself.

Pursuing clarity sounds a lot like becoming proficient in the use of language. Neither are direct paths to achieving the recognizable style or voice we so love in other writers, but whoever said the path to great writing was direct?

Clarity notwithstanding, it's never safe or predictable to turn ourselves loose on the page. Our thoughts and lives and excursions and experiences can become self-indulgent, precious to us, too narrow a gate for even one reader to squeeze through if we're not careful. We become so enamored by the sound of our voice that we resemble E.B. White's self-liberated essayist, "sustained by the childish belief that everything he thinks about, everything that happens to him, is of general interest." Today, we easily see that happening with some bloggers, or even in others' use of social media. (Not ours, of course, but sometimes in theirs.) These modern tools are like catnip to the essayist who is always culling from the miscellany of daily life. If we resist on social media or in blog posts ("too self-indulgent!"), we should eschew the same in our essays.

Instead, we have hard work to do, says Donna Talarico, publisher and managing editor of *Hippocampus*. We must resist the temptation to believe every deeply personal piece we write "will matter to everyone as much as it does" to us. Instead, we have to always be aware of the reader, to remember that "to be published is to entertain—or at least interest—a reader." One way to do that, suggests Sanders, involves not merely calling on the self to know and do things, but also allowing the self to look around, to observe, to engage with the world where readers live. By drawing on the internal *and* external, the essayist transcends herself.

That outward glance on the part of the narrator is what makes personal essays different from autobiography, Sanders reminds us. The famous—and infamous—amass great followings by simply looking inward at the minutiae of their lives.

Their antics, their travels, their hobbies, even their diets fill the pages of autobiographies and are grabbed off shelves and consumed by eager masses of readers looking for the latest scandalous detail. About his private life, though, Sanders assumes the public doesn't give a hoot. So why write in the first person at all, then?

"I choose to write about my experience not because it is mine," Sanders says, "but because it seems to me a door through which others might pass."

~

My essay "A House for Birds" wasn't quite there when I sent it to *Curator Magazine*. Even *I* knew it, as evidenced by my apology couched within the cover letter. But what was missing? I wasn't sure. The three editors who looked at it weren't sure either, but they all suggested that perhaps the story needed a little looking outward, a transcendent moment when, as one editor put it, "the author brings [her] head up out of it for a bit and looks around."

Sometimes, simply switching between the past and present and writing about the same situation with the benefit of hindsight does the trick. Sometimes, you can pull in a quotation or a song lyric or a movie reference, any cultural artifact that allows for the reflective pause—at which point the reader himself can be the prairie dog, lifting his head out of the text to reorient himself to where he is and what the landscape holds.

As for "A House for Birds," it needed a little of all three. After popping up a few times from the story of myself and plopping in a few quotes from an essay that had fed my psyche on the subject I was writing about, I gave the reader everything I could to help him walk through the door my experiences had opened.

Like a lot of my life, writing feels like a frequent U-turn from the highly impersonal towards the self-indulgent. I overcorrect for one extreme and point squarely to the other. At times it's painful to write about what's going on in my world. Sometimes it's too personal: the intersection of my life and others' lives can create a complex network of trusts that must be maintained. Other times, the telling of the minutiae of my day-to-day feels narcissistic. So I hold back. But in those essays where even just a small part of my true self finds its way to the page, I meet the reader and open a gate to invite her to recognize a new bit of herself, too.

When "what somebody's telling you about themselves is not something that you want to hear," we dismiss it as narcissism, says music professor John Covach. He marks Bob Dylan's "warbly first-person anthems" in the 1960s, which fellow folk singer Pete Seeger called narcissistic, as a turning point towards "the dawn of another era characterized by hand-wringing over self-centered youth." But there is a way to write or sing about oneself that isn't perceived that way, Covach says. "[I]f someone is saying something that happened to them and it resonates with your own experience, then you don't call it narcissistic. You call it poetry."

Sometimes, essayists make the best poets.

9

Finding the Funny

"It doesn't matter what happens to Cousin Ron," my stepson told me one day, "he always tells it so funny."

"He's a good storyteller," I agreed.

"He's hysterical," Jacob emphasized. After all, it's one thing to tell a good tale, but it's another to spin it with humor and aplomb.

Ron is my stepsons' relative, but I've spent enough time with him to know what Jacob's talking about. Unique aphorisms, clever voice transformations, understated wit, and a few unbelievable experiences: Ron is the whole humorous package.

Recently, Jacob said a similar thing about our dog. "Tilly is just so funny, even if she's just sitting there." Granted, part of Tilly's routine is the hysterical voiceovers we do for her, giving her all our own fears, hang-ups, and insecurities in the things "she" says. Since that one stay in the local kennel when she contracted kennel cough, we've construed Tilly's voice to sound like a cross between Rachael Ray and Clint Eastwood— low, raspy, *cowboy* with a hint of *gal*.

Tilly's humor also results from her nervous, twitchy "sit," which she reluctantly does on command; the dopey look she gets when she knows we're talking about her; and the "I'm part of the action" gestures she makes when we gather around the dinner table. I can't tell you how many laughs we've gotten from that girl.

"Imagine if Cousin Ron and Tilly were together," I said one evening when I was telling Jacob goodnight.

"We'd never stop laughing," he said.

That's how I feel when I read great humor writing—like I'll never stop laughing. It's not necessarily hysterical; not everyone can be Cousin Ron (and that might be a good thing, especially from Ron's perspective). Sometimes the chuckle takes me by surprise, prompted by a funny line in an otherwise sober essay. But once the laughing starts, I'm ready for more. Any little pun, irony, or exaggeration is likely to get me going again.

I started reading humorist Dave Barry back when he was a syndicated columnist for *The Miami Herald*. I bought his books (really just compilations of his columns) and spent hours at home alone chuckling to myself. It wasn't that I wanted to write like him—I never dreamed I could. But I wanted *him* to keep writing. And though I lost track of him for years, I recently discovered that he fulfilled my wish. Dave Barry's still writing, and his humor is still over the top. He says things the rest of us are thinking. He takes objects and incidents from normal life and pushes them to their logical (or illogical) conclusions. And then he includes a little twist at the end.

When I'm writing funny—and sadly, that's less often than I'd like—I could probably be accused of trying a little too hard to be like Dave Barry. But it's not that I'm trying to copy his style; it's that I find his style of humor so delicious. Amy Poehler, too. When I read her memoir, *Yes, Please,* I recognized elements of Barry there. (Not that I'm saying Poehler is copying Dave. That's my trick.) Of course she's known more for her improvisational comedy from *Saturday Night Live* and her situational comedy in *Parks and Recreation*. But her humor writing is lots of fun, too.

And crude. Half the time I was reading *Yes, Please,* my laughter was actually more nervous than hysterical. I feared Steve or the boys would look over my shoulder while I was reading, especially that one chapter called "My World-Famous Sex Advice," and realize what I was giggling at. Still, like Dave, Amy writes about everyday things in everyday ways until BOOM, she's turned it on me. Surprise. I'm laughing. And I can't stop. Just add Cousin Ron and Tilly, and *I'd* become certifiably hysterical—laughing, that is. (Then my family might start doing voiceovers for *me.*)

I bought *Yes, Please* after I decided to try harder to write funny. Sound like a losing proposition? Some of the funniest writers say it is. E.B. White once claimed that analyzing humor is all but pointless. "Humor can be dissected, as a frog can," he remarked, "but the thing dies in the process and the innards are discouraging to any but the pure scientific mind." So, with trepidation, I entered my little quest to find the funny. But I also toted along a little hope, thanks to a friend.

"I didn't know you were funny," she recently told me after we spent the day together.

"Most people don't," I admitted. We'd been laughing the whole time we were together, but since she knows me mostly from online—and since I rarely write funny—my humorous side had gotten lost.

My particular style of humor—what I call "situational" humor, or "you had to be there"—doesn't translate well on the page. But when I began digging online for some help writing funny, I found an article by Siobhan Adcock titled "Why Every Writer Should Take a Humor Writing Class." Her basic premise? I could learn to be funny…with a lot of work.

"Humor is rigorous stuff," she writes. "Taking apart a funny piece of writing in search of the gears and levers and clown-noses that make it tick is one of the best ways to learn how to write almost anything well, or better."

She had me at clown-noses.

The most important element of humor is surprise, Adcock says. Dave Barry had already taught me that. So had the Indiana Department of Revenue when they erroneously sent me a $500 tax bill a year ago. I wasn't laughing immediately, of course. But still.

The key is to convince your readers, I mean really convince them, that you're going in one direction, then suddenly switch gears, do a 180, and surprise them. For instance, after I told off the DOR employee I had called, she kindly explained that the tax problem was my own fault. Now that was surprising…and eventually pretty funny.

Adcock's second point struck deeper: writing funny is harder than writing sad. What? I didn't believe it at first, because I think about how easily I start laughing when I glance over at Tilly and see her giving me that questioning eye. How hard can it be? But the humor in the moment isn't the humor on the page. And while sad things are just sad, making "not funny" things (or things that are funny only at the time) sound funny later—well, that's hard. And if Adcock is right, what am I doing trying to *write funny*, anyway?

Here's the good news: humor writing is about 90 percent technique. At least that's what Adcock claims. And director

Harold Ramis says that in market research for new television comedies, producers feel successful if about 30 percent of people think a show is funny. Granted, that means if I do everything right, I might still be only 90 percent funny to just three out of ten people who aren't giving me a questioning eye.

So, what techniques make up the 90 percent? Not everyone agrees. (No surprise there.) But I've boiled it down to six principles: exaggeration (or hyperbole), understatement, juxtaposition of opposites (aka incongruence), the rule of three, snowballing, and conflict

Exaggeration is part of most humor. Take a normal incident—like having a bowl of spaghetti—and then multiply it by a thousand. "There I was, eating my thousandth bowl of spaghetti for the day …" Or take that bowl of spaghetti and exaggerate one aspect of it. "I eat so much spaghetti Chef Boyardee applied to be my personal chef."

Understatement, of course, is the opposite. I could use it when I spill spaghetti down the front of my blouse. After wiping at it and making the stain even bigger, I could say, "There, it's hardly noticeable."

The juxtaposition of opposites puts two disparate things together, like serving a giant plate of spaghetti and meatballs to one guest, and a single spaghetti noodle to the other. It would also be funny to put Tilly, with her bad habit of jumping, next to a miniature poodle, properly coiffed and sitting primly next to her. Or for that matter, Tilly eating a dog bowl of spaghetti next to Cousin Ron eating a dinner plate of spaghetti might also elicit a few chuckles.

The rule of three is pretty straightforward. Anytime you

make a list, include three items. Only there's a catch. "List two expected items, then deviate preposterously for the third," explains Teddy Wayne in his *New York Times* essay "Dissecting a Frog: How to Write a Humor Piece." You might say something like, "My daily health regimen consists of purified cold water, warm organic veggies … and hot-pink Hostess Sno Balls" (like the ones I used to take for lunch on field trips back in elementary school).

Speaking of Sno Balls, snowballing occurs when the humor gets bigger and more sophisticated throughout the piece (or even throughout your entire body of work). One version of comedic snowballing suggests that the jokes that worked at the beginning might not work as well in the end. You've explained them already. We get it. We want you to move on. We want the jokes to be bigger, better. In the other snowballing camp are the comics who keep doing the same thing over and over in different contexts with slightly different emphases. The sheer repetition—the refusal to stop—creates a snowball effect that just keeps rolling.

When I was in college, I had a philosophy professor who lectured in a rather cavernous classroom using a microphone. For each class session, he came in wearing tennis shoes, dress slacks, and a buttoned-down Oxford over a printed T-shirt. He would walk to the front of the room, drop his briefcase on the table next to the lectern, and pop open his can of Diet Pepsi directly in front of the microphones. "Fsssssss."

The first time we laughed. The second time we laughed. The third time we snickered. And then we just ignored him. But he kept doing it. Every class session. The printed T-shirt, the dress Oxford, the Diet Pepsi. The "Fsssss." By the 27th time or so, we started laughing again. "He's still doing it!" And then we kept laughing, the humor snowballing as he kept doing the same thing ad infinitum, ad absurdum.

You could say that I've been snowballing in this chapter. If I say the words "Cousin Ron" or "Tilly" or "spaghetti," you might smile to yourself because of my sheer tenacity. Of course, you might also do a 180 (and stop reading), because how could someone with as little capacity for on-page humor as me teach you anything about writing funny anyway?

Speaking of which, conflict is also part of good humor writing. When my husband and I listen to Pandora's PG Comedy channel with the boys, I'm always struck by how many comedians, mostly men, capitalize on the conflict between spouses. But it works every time. Conflicts between parents and kids also seem to be big in the comedy world, though as a parent, I'm not always sure I should be laughing. Especially in front of the boys.

There are a few other techniques to humor writing that probably also fall in that 90 percent. All of the following can make your writing funny: making yourself the butt of a joke (I have an almost bottomless love for this), comedic timing (ending the joke—or essay, in our case—with the punch line), and being specific ("hot-pink Sno Balls" instead of "cream-filled snack cakes").

Not everyone is inclined towards humor writing. Some of us (ahem … *me*) will find that the harder we try to be funny, the harder we'll have to try. But probably the biggest surprise of all is that most us are already funny and we didn't even know it.

Apparently that's the case with Cousin Ron. "He doesn't

even *try* to be funny," Jacob told me the other day. "He just *is*." With a little practice, a lot heart, and a handful of hot-pink Sno Balls, that might become true of us someday, too.

10

When It All Falls Apart

This is the way it always goes.

I work on an essay for weeks, maybe months. When I get to the end, relief settles over me. The hard work's over, I tell myself. I move the to-do card to my Trello DONE list, and my brain releases a quick burst of dopamine. I feel lighter, happier. So happy. My inner self spins around in circles like Will Ferrell as Buddy the Elf. "I'm done, I'm done, and I don't care who knows it!" I begin to envision my essay laid out in the thick, smooth pages of a magazine or staring up at me from the screen of an online venue. I think about the next project, confidence pulsing through me, and I am sure the final barriers between me and critical acclaim have finally been lifted.

Then the dopamine dissipates, and I'm facing a rough draft that needs major revisions. No matter how good I felt just moments ago, I'm not done, and I know it.

If I can, I set the work aside for a day or two. Then I go back to the essay and revise. And revise and revise and revise. Sometimes, even after extensive changes, the whole project feels out of balance. I put it aside again, this time for as long as possible. When I pull it back out, I read it slowly, as if for the first time. Before I get far at all, I begin to see the problem. *That's not right.* I change a word or two. *Wait, what if I …* I add a comma, replace a colon with a dash, divide a sentence. Sometimes I rearrange paragraphs or add more details. More often than that, I "omit needless words." Strunk and White would be proud.

Before the first word is written, writers must know—and come to terms with—the fact that revision is part of the process. In fact, Klinkenborg says, "All writing is revision." Sometimes, that first draft will be pretty good, but is it good enough? I don't want to settle. On the other hand, writers who try too hard to make the first draft perfect may actually suppress their best writing. Alice LaPlante says that the desire for immediate perfection "raises the odds that a writer will freeze and/or go abstract, rather than focusing on the small telling details that will eventually lead to riveting and important material." Let's not put that kind of pressure on ourselves. It probably won't be perfect anyway. Plan on revisions.

As important as this part of the process is, not many writers I know feel comfortable revising their work. Part of it is a misconception: Some people think revision is simply proofreading, and they're not good with commas. Others think they're too close to the work to see its problems. And while that can be true, that doesn't mean self-revision isn't necessary. Perhaps our worst aversion to self-editing is the inability to "Murder [our] darlings." We grow to love our argument and that certain turn of phrase, and we can't bear to make any changes for fear it will ruin the whole. (Now you know the writing worry that keeps me up at night!)

One of the initial elements I look at when I return to my essays is the order. First, the scenes, summary, and exposition. Then the order of the paragraphs and how well they transition from one to the next. Finally, the order of the sentences and the way each connects to the next. While order is not always a problem, if something seems off it's usually because I've not presented the pieces in the right sequence to help the reader follow my inquiry or understand my meaning.

For example, just as memoir or fiction has a narrative arc or plot, with growing conflict, a tumultuous climax, and a satisfying resolution, essays also have trajectory that builds and grows. Though I try to avoid endings that wrap things up too tidily, I want to at least leave my reader with a gratifying conclusion. Helping the reader arrive at that destination depends on the essay's structure. In my own first drafts, I'm often guilty of telling the reader right away where I'm headed, when a bit of inquiry or a carefully-written scene can serve as a more intriguing start. Also, while conclusions in logic seem like they belong in the conclusion of my essay, that's usually not the case. I like to turn those big ideas on their heads, so moving them to the middle of my essay, where I can pivot from one direction to another, makes more sense. Finally, one of the last moves I often make is to take a bit of the story that began the essay and return to it at the end. This brings readers back to the narrative that captured their attention in the first place.

Once I fix the structural issues, I can focus on how the essay sounds.

When I first began to publish my work, I had no idea what my writing voice sounded like. When I was a young journalist, readers would comment that my stories sounded different from others in our paper. *It's like you're sitting across the table talking to me*, they'd say. One gentleman told me he could always tell I was the author before ever reading my byline because he recognized the way I wrote. I began to explore the differences between my work and my colleagues'.

Later, when my work was featured in a national magazine, I first received back a revised version of my article. The editors invited me to review the essay to be sure they hadn't changed the meaning or put words in my mouth. I didn't question a single edit, at least not on the basis they had suggested. However, I did feel the writing no longer sounded like me, and it bothered me. After publishing a few articles with them, I found ways to adapt to their style while also retaining my voice.

Revising my work to highlight my unique voice is an area I continue to grow in. First, I'm learning to identify my pet word choices and grammar anomalies, not so I can use them more but so I can use them more carefully. For instance, I love using parenthetical elements set off with dashes or even ellipses. The technique allows for some of the point/counterpoint writing I find so exciting in essays. But including parenthetical elements set off with dashes in every sentence is exhausting for the reader. When I revise, I find ways to include this device only when it will be most effective.

Another aspect of my writing that I continue to work on is integrating quotations and information from outside sources with my own thoughts. I tend to read widely and make broad connections among the events and articles and podcasts I experience, so my essays can be filled to the brim with what others have to say. Too often I let them do the talking, and my first drafts fill with long passages from books and essays; upon revision, I need to tease out just the most vibrant elements to weave with my words. Rather than using block-quotes, which I love, I push myself towards embedded quotes, where what is quoted and what I write on my own sound like a seamless sentence … except, of course, for the quotation marks and cited endnotes.

Finally, I revise to achieve the rhythm I hear in my head. This one is harder, but when it comes to allowing my voice to emerge, it's essential. Often, revising for rhythm means I cut out words that are slowing things down. I also swap out words to be more precise, and I aim for active verbs and concrete nouns that eliminate the need for adjectives and adverbs, though there's nothing wrong with a well-placed modifier here or there. When I see them—because they can be sneaky little elements—I remove most of the *thats* and the *-ings*. But here's my surprising little secret: occasionally I'll add some of those back in if they improve the rhythm and make my essay sound more like me.

Finally, even when I do everything right, my revisions will take my writing only up to a point, so I appreciate the feedback of others to really help my writing hum. I'm not talking about the work of the editor to whom I'll submit my essay. I'm talking about the fellow writer I ask to read over my work, or even the freelance editor I hire to review my essay before I send it to a publisher. Anytime I get input from a reader or editor prior to submitting my work for publication, I need to understand where I am in the writing process in order to ask for and receive the proper feedback. (Check out Appendix B for more tips on asking for and getting feedback from others.)

In the early stages of drafting or having completed just a first draft, asking for feedback may do more harm than good. I may not have the pieces of my essay in the right order yet, and to have someone critique my work could be discouraging or even damaging to the creative process. If I do ask for feedback in these early stages, I should simply ask the reader to tell me what's working. Then, as I do my own revisions, I can build from there.

Later in the process, I might ask a reader to identify problems I can't see because I'm too close to the work. Does the inquiry build and resolve as I expect? Are there any terms or concepts that haven't been defined or explained? Are my characters believable? Have I answered all the questions the reader has about setting?

Finally, when I've gone through several revisions and feel the work is nearly ready to send, that's when I can ask for a copyedit or a proofread to help with spelling and typos and syntax. This is the perfect time to have a friend whose list of skills includes "attention to detail."

One final tool worth mentioning is what Alice LaPlante calls "exercise-based revision." Instead of having early readers tell us how to solve the problems in our writing, we can write through the problems "in the margins." This extra writing may not end up in the final draft, but it helps us understand what's needed.

In *The Making of a Story*, LaPlante uses the example of a mother and daughter whose relationship seems underdeveloped. Rather than expect the reader to come up with how to fix the problem, she suggests that the writer could use exercises to explore what's needed. For instance, she could "write five vignettes of the last five times the mother and daughter disagreed," which may better reveal the dynamic between the characters that was missing in the essay.

Doing exercise-based revision avoids the Band-Aid approach of using someone else's advice to fix problem areas.

Instead, it puts "a metaphorical stick of dynamite there, to explode the piece in a way that teaches you more, and more interesting, things about the piece than you were previously aware." This approach also helps us understand the problems in our writing before we tear apart the essay trying to fix it. Revision can be a challenging process. Exercise-based revision, when it's time, can make that process easier.

Because I enjoy that dopamine rush that comes with crossing off a completed first draft from my to-do list, I usually add a separate line item for revisions now, too. At some point, often with a deadline staring me down, I'll decide I've finally finished my essay, and I'll cross that item off the list too. *There*, I'll say, already feeling the tension between my shoulder blades ease up just a bit. And, for a few minutes at least, I'll actually believe the process is complete.

11

Finishing

"Did you hear Shaun White won?" I asked my husband, who was reading on the couch after supper.

He glared at me.

"Oh, sorry. Were you planning to watch the Olympics tonight?"

"I was," he said, now smiling. "It's okay. I'll still watch."

I'd been driving home from a client meeting when I heard the news that White had won the US's 100th gold medal in Pyeongchang and reclaimed his title as king of the half-pipe competition. Because of the time difference, the competition wouldn't actually be broadcast until that night, even though the results had already been thoroughly reported.

The victory was an amazing comeback for the athlete who had been dubbed the "Flying Tomato" early in his career because of his floppy mop of red hair. He'd been favored to win four years earlier during the Sochi games, but ended up placing fourth. Steve and I watched that competition on delay, too, and like this time, we already knew the results. That's partly why we had tuned in; it was a major upset in the 2014 games.

The ride that cost White a medal that year included a trick he'd practiced and perfected, a cab double cork 1440, known as a "YOLO flip." After the results were tallied, White told ESPN, "I hate the fact I nailed it in practice, but it happens.

It's hard to be consistent."

The 2018 competition was completely different. Since White's defeat in 2014, the level of competition had grown more intense. A rider from Japan, Ayumu Hirano, had won the X Games just weeks before Pyeongchang, doing a series of tricks White himself had never performed in competition: a YOLO flip preceded by a front-side double cork 1440.

When it was time for White's final ride—which was also the final ride of the competition—he'd fallen behind Hirano. In order to win, White would have to land the back-to-back 1440s, plus nail the rest of his ride. The crowds watched as White executed a nearly flawless performance. When the score of 97.75 was announced, he knew he'd won gold.

"Honestly, it's one of the most challenging runs I've ever done," he told NBC Sports afterwards. "I didn't even link the combination, the 14 to 14, until I got here, today, this morning. So, honestly, I'm just so happy with my performance. I'm proud of the other riders for pushing me this whole time."

No one questions the enormous successes White has achieved. But the breakout wonder didn't get as far as he has without being knocked down a few times. Of course there was the loss in Sochi, but in the years leading up to the 2014 Olympics, White also experienced a series of personal setbacks. In 2012, he was arrested for public intoxication and suffered a minor head injury. By that time he also had developed a reputation of being a "selfish jerk" who refused to allow other snowboarders to train at his personal half-pipe built for him by Red Bull prior to the 2010 Olympics. More recently, White was severely injured during a competition in New Zealand while attempting one of those 1440s. He received 62 stitches.

It's no wonder that he had at times questioned whether he should continue. It's also no wonder that he broke down in tears when he found himself back on top again.

White's story offers an important parallel to the writing life, especially when we're standing with a finished essay in hand, expectant with all the possibility that might come with it. Sure, we can want the gold-medal level of success that White has achieved, but it doesn't come without the hard work, disappointments, and failures that White also experienced. We have to be willing to experience and expect a little of each if we want to make it in the writing business. It also means we need a plan that includes more than just an exception clause in a publishing industry that's notoriously difficult to break into. Some of us will become wildly successful against all odds. But it's foolish to stake a whole career on such a wild bet.

Several years ago, I completed a draft of a book I had been working on for years and whipped up a book proposal just in time for a writers' conference I was attending. Though I realize now that the proposal wasn't as good as it could have been, I got the attention of a small publisher. They liked my idea! They would get back with me.

But they didn't. Not for months. The wait was torturous. The writing I did during that time was stunted. When I finally learned that they would be passing on my book, I didn't write at all for months. It wasn't that this one book deal would have sealed my career as a writer, but I had acted as if it would. I had no backup plan, no contingencies. The one rejection nearly sidelined me.

This past year, I had a similar experience. A book proposal I'd developed landed on the desk of another publisher who expressed similar interest. Just like that publisher years ago, they told me they'd get back to me and didn't. Not for months. And as expected, the wait was equally torturous. But this time, I had a plan B. I was already working on other things. I didn't stake my whole career on this one response. If they said yes, I'd be elated. If they said no, I'd keep ticking away at all the other books and essays and articles I was working on. Which is exactly what happened when the publisher eventually passed. I was disappointed, but not crushed. Not this time. I'd learned from that earlier rejection.

That's the beauty of small early rejections: they can teach us the hard knocks of the writing life if we let them. Developing survival methods for the small "no's" can help us navigate the larger ones, when the risks are greater and the stakes are higher. Each of us will develop our own methods, but, generally, dealing well with rejection requires three things: realistic expectations (rejections *will* come); reasonable plans B, C, and D for the projects we put a lot of effort into (don't let one rejection keep you from sending your work out again); and relationships with other people (possibly other writers) that can help ease us through the hard times.

Regarding those B-C-D plans, we can look back to White: snowboarding isn't his only passion. He's involved in so many different projects, in fact, that in 2011, he created Shaun White Enterprises as a way to consolidate all of his business and philanthropic interests. He lends his name—maybe "leases" is more like it—to clothing lines and snowboarding accessories. He produced a documentary about himself. He's played lead guitar in a band called Bad Things. He's the owner of an *Air + Style Show* franchise. And of course he still competes.

His secret to soaring success both on and off the slopes? A good strategy.

"The whole strategizing thing is what does it for me," White told Elizabeth Weil in a *New York Times* interview. "That's what I do on the hill. I'm always thinking: Well, if this could happen, then that could happen. It'll leave me in this position, it'll create these opportunities."

The same is true for the writing life. In addition to a little serendipity, a life of words benefits from having a blueprint. If my goal is simply to write, I could spend a lifetime of words just on my own blog, writing whatever I wish. In fact, if I don't even want an audience, I could just buy a journal and get to work. But if I would like to have some readers, gather a few publishing credits, earn an income, or possibly hit the bestseller list, then I need a strategy.

What does having a strategy look like in your own writing life? How will you decide whether to stick with your first passion—like White and *skateboarding*—or move on to another genre—like White and *snowboarding?* And at what point should you push for your own clothing line? If athletes can have clothing lines, why not authors? (I'm looking at you, Zadie Smith.)

A good strategy starts with goals. Of course, they'll change and grow over time, just like you ... and your writing. But, as of today, what are your goals? Do you want to write only for yourself? Does "publish" mean making ten copies of your recent essay and passing them around to the people you know? Are the posts on your blog enough? Do the people who come for the words there represent your ideal readership? If so, then you're on your way.

Alternately, are you looking to gather publishing credits from other blogs, websites, and magazines? Are you looking to publish in a certain kind of publication—maybe a literary journal instead of a magazine? Are you hoping to make some money in the process? Since you've made it this far in a book about writing essays, I'll assume that you'd like to *publish* essays, though that's likely not the whole of your writing ambition. Eventually, you may also want to consider goals for your poetry, fiction, music reviews, or memoir.

Once you've identified your goals, begin to look for publishers to whom you can send your work. First, look at the publications (or publishers, for longer writing) you already read. Because you're familiar with their work, you'll know their audience (hint: it's you and people like you) and their style. Don't forget to look for possible publications in the portfolio section of other writers' websites, too, particularly writers who are doing work similar to yours. Look there for new magazines, new publishers, and new markets to expand your pool. In Appendix B, I offer a list of resources to help you find places to send your essays.

After you've determined where to send your work, review the submission guidelines for the publication. I can't cover all the rules for sending out your work, because each publication has its own specific guidelines. However, here are a few rules of thumb:

• Don't submit to a publication without familiarizing yourself with previous essays they've published. Also, read through their guidelines to see what kind of work the publisher is requesting. If they don't accept personal essays, don't send them yours.

• Follow a publisher's guidelines precisely, including word counts and deadlines. Don't assume you or your work can be an exception.

• Give publishers your best work at every point in the process. If you're asked for a query letter, send it in with your best, most professional writing. Revise and proofread each email, each synopsis, each pitch. Your writing is being evaluated, even before editors get their hands on your essays.

Keep track of the work you send, logging acceptances and rejections. If you do get a rejection, consider any feedback the publisher provided—or look again yourself for any further revisions—and then send it out again. If you get an acceptance, well, you know what to do. (I would suggest Kool & the Gang's "Celebration" along with a funky victory dance.)

Even if your essay is accepted, chances are it will come back to you at least once before it's published, now marked up with comments and suggested changes from your editor, which will send you back to the revision process, this time trying to align with someone else's vision for your work.

If I could, I'd spare you this last stretch of the essay writing process. For me, it might be the hardest part of all. Though it means someone said yes to my essay, it's another reminder that I still haven't arrived. I'm still not able to write the "perfect" essay. No matter how hard I try or how much time I spend, I'll always need someone else's help to do the work of writing.

But maybe that's okay. Maybe this realization is actually one motivation I need to keep writing. And maybe, as Louise DeSalvo writes, "understanding that our work can never meet our expectations can help us let go of it, and can allow us to move on to the next phase of our writing lives."

Having goals, but also being willing to move on for any number of reasons and at every stage of the process—hopefully with a little encouragement from a few good writing friends: this can help us nail the rest of our wild writing ride.

And I'd be happy to tune in to *yours* sometimes, if I know when and where I can find you making your way.

12

Writing What Matters

The July/August 2015 issue of *The Atlantic* listed a series of "ideas of the year" or "intellectual trends that, for better or for worse, are informing the national conversation and shaping our lives."

Some of them were funny: "Old People Are Cool" or "The Long National Night of Cable TV Is Over" or "The NFL Is Evil—and Unstoppable." Well, at least they're funny as in not-as-serious-as-the-rest, because many of the other ideas of 2015 were not funny at all. Like the one that suggests "The Cold War Never Ended" or right next to that, ironically, "Americans Are Okay with Surveillance and Torture." The list left out very little, adding the campus sexual-assault crisis, racism, global religious intolerance, and economic inequality to the ideas our nation was talking about that year.

Many of these 2015 trending ideas are still trending today, and while the conversation may have shifted, the topics we're talking about aren't all that new. But there's a problem. One item on that list may actually be keeping us from making any progress on the others, and it's the most disheartening of all: "There will be no debate."

"A proper argument takes intellectual vigor, nimbleness, and sustained attention," author Hanna Rosin asserts. "If carried on long enough, it can push both parties to a deeper level of understanding. Oxford debaters hack away at each other for something like two hours. Socrates could sometimes go on for weeks. But who has that kind of time anymore?"

Rosin goes on to explain our society's unmistakable loss of appetite when it comes to debating, or even just discussing, the issues of the day. Where do essays, with their big ideas and nuanced thinking, even fit in a culture that refuses to listen?

In the past couple of years, I can't count the number of times I've seen friends write a few thoughts on Facebook, an online essay, or a blog post, only to be met with hateful comments and emails that harshly close, instead of gently open, debate. We could blame the political climate; the level of vitriol certainly seems high in recent years. We could also blame social media. And certainly social media may be at least partly to blame. But maybe this trend began long before we all began to think in 280 characters or less. That's what Wendell Berry suggests.

"My impression is that we have seen, for perhaps a hundred and fifty years, a gradual increase in language that is either meaningless or destructive of meaning," Berry wrote back in 1979 in his essay "Standing by Words." He contends that the loss of meaningful language parallels about two centuries of disintegration of meaningful community in the U.S. The result, Berry says, is a lack of accountability—of both language and its users.

If Berry is correct, the only way to redeem language and restore debate is to hold the users of language accountable for what they say, to move them towards a use of words that builds up rather than tears down. Berry calls this a "precision" of language that is otherwise missing in our handling of words.

One way we achieve this precision is by choosing words

that come from a shared knowledge of places, vocations, history, and more, what Berry calls "community speech." When we use language we all understand and agree on, we don't get stuck wrangling over the definition of specific words. Instead, we connect more meaningfully with each other by insisting on context and joining ongoing conversations. Words mean something more specifically when they are part of a greater story.

But Berry's other path towards precision poses a greater challenge for those of us for whom "there will be no debate." This other type of word use exists in the "tension either between a statement and a prepared context or, within a single statement, between more or less conflicting feelings or ideas," he writes. It's holding two different ideas in one hand and saying "both/and" rather than "either/or." It's dismissing generalities because rarely is something all bad or all good.

As essayists, we have a choice. We can either perpetuate the imprecision and lack of dialogue, using language that is meaningless and destructive, or we can participate in genuine conversations with people we may not agree with and work towards precision of language.

Writing this way accomplishes several things. Using a shared community language invites us to listen and adapt to the conversation already in progress, requires us to define new words or concepts we introduce and wait for them to be accepted by others, and transforms words from weapons into tools. Writing in context means our ideas are not divorced from the real activities of the world; we aren't just speaking theoretically. And writing with specificity and tension means we don't create false dichotomies. We are loath to rely on stereotypes or characterizations that don't actually exist.

For my own part, I like to avoid arguing as much as the next person. But too often I get lazy with the words I write, and I expect others to just *know what I mean*, regardless of how I say it. In fact, I was laughing with family recently about an invention of the future that would do just that: a scrolling display attached to my forehead that would explain my real meaning when I get tongue-tied or fogged up in my thoughts.

Or I could hold myself accountable to a better rhetoric, to a more ambitious (in the best sense of the word) use of language. Rather than avoiding a debate or shutting it down, I could start by listening and then entering the conversation with the precision that reflects the larger community and ongoing narrative I find myself a part of.

But there's a final point Berry makes about what it means to be accountable for our language, one that's far more sobering to consider. He says that in order for a statement to be complete and comprehensible, its speaker must stand by it— "must believe it, be accountable for it, be willing to act on it."

If that's the standard, what would I ever be willing to write?

Writers of every genre can take up the banner of standing by their words, but essayists particularly have an opportunity to write beyond meaning towards *what really matters*. If we employ a thread to run through our work, it's a thread we can tug on to determine the meaning of our stories and vignettes and quotations and exposition. But we can't be satisfied with just a pretty thread collection. We need our threads to connect to others, to be woven into patterns and designs. Does anyone pull wool just to make a pretty spool? Maybe. But usually there's a bigger goal: to create a garment to cover us, protect us, and express who we are when we leave the house.

Our essays don't just *have* meaning. They must *mean something* to us and to the world around us. Essayists can occupy a particular role in society, next to poets and novelists. We can gather bits of conversations and evidence of events around us. We can interpret them in new ways, connecting them together as we write. Then, pulling from our own lives, we can write "as a person," one who is asking questions and forming opinions and offering another way, maybe even a better way, to see things. We don't "write in order to win sympathy or praise," as Scott Russell Sanders says. Instead, we "write to share understanding about the human struggle, and to share delight in the power of language." This is how we move from speculation past narcissism towards embodied critical thinking. This is how we stand by words.

When neurologist and acclaimed author Oliver Sacks died, a *New York Times* obituary mentioned his published writings, many of which focused on his patients' disorders. Some critics felt he exploited those he was duty-bound to serve. Fellow scientists felt he mishandled clinical evidence in favor of stories, and London neuroscientist Ray Dolan told *The Guardian* in 2005 that he "always felt uncomfortable about this side of this work, and especially the tendency for Dr. Sacks to be an ever-present dramatis persona."

Sacks thought of his work differently, though. He felt his role was to listen, not only to his patients but to all he encountered. "I've tried to imagine what it was like for them, and that I tried to convey this. And, to use a biblical term, bore witness," he said in a 1989 interview on *The MacNeil Lehrer News-*

Hour on PBS.

It is a lofty undertaking to bear witness. The tide rises and falls on justices and injustices. Those who can (and do) speak for themselves rise along with it. But at times it's primarily the writers—the poets, the novelists, the essayists—who stand not only by our words, but also by other people—even *in place of* other people—who can't speak for themselves.

This can make us unwelcome because of our inquiry, our speculations, our ideas, and we may experience a cost. But we may experience rewards, too. Anne Lamott says it best in *Bird by Bird:* "Being a writer is part of a noble tradition, as is being a musician—the last egalitarian and open associations. No matter what happens in terms of fame and fortune, dedication to writing is a marching-step forward from where you were before."

I say this to myself, then, even as I say it to you: Take up the noble tradition, Writer. These are your marching orders. Stand up and write. Stand by your words.

Epilogue: Next

When I worked as a reporter in the mid-1990s, we were a late afternoon newspaper, which meant our deadlines fell sometime mid-morning on the day of publication. By noon, everything had to be written, edited, proofread, and laid out so the plates could be made and the presses run. My stories were usually finished around 10 a.m., but I stuck around until noon when I saw them printed, trimmed, and glued down on the page. That's when I knew I was done. I celebrated by heading home for my lunch break.

The regular grind of producing a daily paper left little time for festivity, and if I didn't immediately get started on the next story, I'd never meet the following day's deadline. In the same way I couldn't afford the time to process the emotional attachment I developed with each story, I couldn't worry how my work would be received in the world. I couldn't mourn the loss of releasing the story and moving on to something new. I had to keep writing.

But where the rhythm of print journalism left no time for me to process, I know now that processing is a necessity for my writing life. I need to take time to celebrate, to enjoy the success of finishing.

In "Make Good Art," his commencement speech to Philadelphia's University of the Arts, writer Neil Gaiman talks about the regret of not celebrating his own early success.

"I didn't stop and look around and go, 'This is really fun.' I wish I'd enjoyed it more. It's been an amazing ride. But there were parts of the ride I missed, because I was too worried about things going wrong, about what came next, to enjoy the bit I was on."

But of course we writers have a complicated relationship with our work, and I suspect the more personal our subject matter, the more complicated that relationship. We come to the writing day after day, slipping tiny fragments of ourselves between the pixels. When we're not actually working, we discover the essay has tucked itself into the hem of our thoughts. It lingers with us when we're quiet; we dream about it when we sleep. We write, we worry, we revise, then we finish. And when we finally have a minute to relax and celebrate, instead, we mourn the loss of what had become such a part of us.

After the mourning comes the misgivings: Will it be loved or will it be rejected? Will it find a home, or will it be stuck in the limbo of so many words that never see publication? Was this my masterpiece? What if I never write as well again?

I've often heard that it takes half as long as a relationship lasted to heal it once it has ended, and I wonder if the same is true for our writing. Not every essay leaves me with such a complicated departure to recover from, especially those that were written and sent off quickly. The books I've written have been harder, weaving a long and intricate thread through my life. For this book, the unwinding may take a whole year.

But whatever loss or dissatisfaction I'm left with at the end of a project, at the very least, I hope to use it to propel me on to what's next. And there will be a next, because I'm not just a creator of an essay, and I'm not just the author of any given book. I'm a writer, living a writing life. And you're a writer, too. For the long haul. As Louise DeSalvo reminds us, "If we see our writing life as a continuum, we can acknowledge that writing each book [or essay] teaches us something that writing no other book [or essay] can, and we can look forward to what we'll learn from the new work awaiting us."

So, though you've come to the end of this book, you've actually arrived once again at a beginning—the beginning of all that's next. Today, we get to start again, taking new risks, suffering new failures, and eventually realizing: the biggest success of the writing life is that we get to live it at all.

Appendix A: Take It Further

Activities for Personal Journals, Classrooms & Writing Groups

Chapter 1 • Listen to the Whispers

RESPOND: Have you ever lost an idea because you didn't take time to capture it? How did it make you feel? Did it return to you later? How did the experience change the way you think about collecting writing ideas?

PRACTICE: If you don't already have a commonplace book, think about how you can incorporate one into your writing life using some of the suggestions in Chapter 1. If you're already in the practice of jotting down ideas, quotations, and other items of interest, brainstorm ways to make your habit more useful. Could you create an index of all your old notebooks? Would it make sense to begin a digital version of your system? What about creating a weekly recurring task on your favorite time management app to review your ideas for further exploration? With your system in place, start or continue to collect items for your commonplace book, including stories, images, quotes, passages, thoughts, and more.

READ: "Write Till You Drop" by Annie Dillard from *The New York Times*, May 28, 1989, about giving your all to your writing, and "On Keeping a Notebook" by Joan Didion from her 1968 anthology *Slouching Towards Bethlehem*, on the author's regular practice of jotting down observations. Both pieces help us think about our life as a well from which most essays are drawn.

What details do these essays include that give you a sense of the authors' lives? What clues are there as to how the authors gathered, stored, and retrieved these details? What advice do the authors offer that seems helpful for your own writing life and process?

Chapter 2 • Memory & Truth

RESPOND: Do you write from memory? What are your hesitations? How do you ensure you are finding and communicating the truth? On the flip side, do you ever worry that you aren't including enough detail to give a clear picture when you write? How do you feel after reading Chapter 2?

PRACTICE: In her essay "'Perhapsing': The Use of Speculation in Creative Nonfiction," Lisa Knopp describes techniques nonfiction writers can use to fill in the gaps of their knowledge of actual events. Using words like "perhaps" or "may have been" or "I imagine," writers can make their best guesses about what someone might have been thinking or what might have happened. Think back to one of your birthdays in the past when you celebrated with other people. Recreate the scene, "perhapsing" where necessary to fill in the gaps of why certain family members were or weren't there, why they chose a certain gift for you, or why you do or don't have any photos to look back on. If you can't think of a birthday, come up with another occasion for which you have only limited details about others' involvement.

READ: "Eat, Memory: Orange Crush" by Yiyun Li from *The New York Times,* January 22, 2006, about an experience from the author's childhood in China, and "Tan Lines" by Durga Chew-Bose from *Medium*, August 17, 2015, about growing up with brown skin during summer when everyone wanted brown skin. These essays will help us think about using memory to feed our essays.

What role do you think memory played in the authors' writing? How much truth do you think the authors found and communicated? Why do you think the authors included the details they did? If these were your stories, how would make them as true as possible?

Chapter 3 • May I Ask?

RESPOND: Do you like to research for your writing? Why or why not? What aspects of research do you embrace? Which parts make you uneasy? Do you tend to lean more heavily on digital or analog sources—and what are the implications of that? How do the ideas of *investigation* and *inquiry* make simple "research" more interesting? Take a few minutes to explore your thoughts in your journal.

Next, list the places you regularly go to find information and perspectives you can trust. What other methods or sources could you experiment with to make your essays richer? Make a list of those, too, and star one or two that you'd consider using in your next project.

PRACTICE: Spend 15 minutes sifting through your commonplace book and find one topic you could write about for your next essay (don't worry, we won't hold you to it). Then ask yourself the 5 Ws and 1 H (who, what, when, where, why, and how) about your idea. You may need to dig a little deeper to find a scenario or a fact to explore. Pay attention to the questions you struggle to answer. How could you go about finding the answers to any of the six elements you don't already know?

READ: "The Black Family in the Age of Mass Incarceration" by Ta-Nehisi Coates for *The Atlantic,* October 2015 issue, an essay about the inequalities of the American prison system and its effect on black Americans, and "The Trash Heap Has Spoken" by Carmen Maria Machado for *Guernica*, February 13, 2017, about fatness and its unacceptability in modern culture. These essays will help us explore how authors' investigations enhance the meaning of their essays.

How would these essays be different if the authors appealed only to emotion without including the factual evidence? How do the authors present their research in a way that intensifies the emotional connection for the reader rather than watering it down?

Chapter 4 • Making Maps

RESPOND: In Chapter 4 we talked about making maps of our essays before we start writing. How do you feel about that strategy? Have you used any of the mapping ideas discussed in this chapter? How did it go? Do you regularly play with ideas, arranging and rearranging them until you recognize the path you need to take? Or do you quickly categorize your ideas into a strict structure? Spend a few minutes free writing in your journal with your answers.

PRACTICE: Try a mind map. Start by writing an idea in the center of a piece of paper and circling it. If you can't think of an idea, try "home" or "work" or some other broad concept. Now, begin thinking of ideas related to your initial word. Write down each idea, circle it, and then draw a line connecting it your original idea. Then keep going, using each circle as an opportunity to drill down into your memory, adding in facts, anecdotes, or related books and articles. As your mind map grows, you might find that one or two sub-ideas begin to show promise for your work. If so, consider pulling them out and starting a new mind map. After you've spent some time playing with your idea, consider developing it into an essay.

READ: "Against Joie de Vivre" by Phillip Lopate in *Against Joie de Vivre: Personal Essays*, Poseidon Press 1989, about getting the most enjoyment out of life, and "I Lift My Lamp" by Peter Trachtenberg for *Scoundrel Time*, January 29, 2017, about immigration, asylum, and exile. Both essays comprise different components that had to be mapped by the author in the writing.

How did the authors piece together these essays? Would the essays mean something different if they had been structured differently? Print the essays and cut them apart by paragraph. Create a train of thought based on the published versions, then rearrange and imagine why the authors arranged the essays the way they did.

Chapter 5 • Show, Tell, Explain

RESPOND: Have you heard the advice to "show, not tell" before? How has that advice shaped the way you write? Have you ever considered that most writing is actually a combination of showing, telling, and explaining? In what ways does your writing reflect that? How different are telling and explaining in your mind? Is there any difference at all? Does it help to use the terms "narrative summary" and "exposition"?

PRACTICE: Let's explore the interplay of showing, telling, and explaining. First, think of a scene that took place in your past. Dig deep into your memory to include as many details as possible, letting one memory shake others loose. In this first draft, don't analyze or critique the events, places, or people you're describing; just tell us what happened. Next, dig deeper. Tell the reader more about the background to this story. Explain why this scene is important by connecting it to what was going on in the world at the time. As you write, be mindful of when you are showing, when you are telling, and when you are explaining.

READ: "Buckeye" by Scott Russell Sanders at Terrain.org, about Sanders' move towards conservationism, and "Drinking Chai to Savannah: Reflections on Identity, Inclusion and Power in the South" by Anjali Enjeti at Longreads.com, January 24, 2017, about a girl's road trip with six of her immigrant friends. Both essays provide great examples of the intersection of the three elements of essay writing discussed in Chapter 5: showing, telling, and explaining.

Print a copy of each essay, and with three different color highlighters, mark them up based on the three elements above. Notice the way the authors intermingle showing, telling, and explaining. Which element is used most often? Do you think the essays would benefit from more balance among the three?

Chapter 6 • Place It

RESPOND: How easy is it for you to use your senses to describe the world around you? Do you rely on one or two and neglect the others? Do you find that you include too many details? Or do you struggle to come up with any descriptions at all? As you move around the spaces you occupy, do you have a sense of place, of what makes this particular place so particular? If so, how do you typically incorporate those into your writing? Spend some time reflecting on the sensory details around you and try to capture a few of those in your journal. And as you fill your commonplace book, look for descriptions of people and places in the reading you're doing that do a good job of evoking a sense of place.

PRACTICE: Think of a place you used to live or work. Now that you are away from it, how would you describe it? Write about an encounter you had in this space and include enough detail about the room, the neighborhood, or the office so that your readers would understand the essence of the place. Now, go back through this short vignette and add more sensory detail, to evoke at least three senses. And include detail that only someone who lived or worked there would know. For instance, instead of using the word "tools," tell us each one's name and what it does.

READ: "Diary (Pale Bus, Pale Rider)" by Rebecca Solnit from *The London Review of Books*, Vol. 36 No. 4 · 20 February 2014, about transportation protests in Silicon Valley, and "Renewing Husbandry" by Wendell Berry from *Orion Magazine*, which discusses the role of husbandry in modern agriculture. In these two essays, the authors not only use place as a background or setting for their writing but also make place integral to the meaning of their essays.

What places is each author writing about? What information does the author tell you about each place? What do the authors assume you know? How would these essays be different if they were about other places?

Chapter 7 • Write Them In

RESPOND: Where do you fall when it comes to writing about the people in your life? Do you write freely, like Anne Lamott suggested, owning your stories and insisting others should have "behaved better" if they wanted to be left out? Or are you more reticent, like Scott Russell Sanders, who published the story of his alcoholic father only after he had permission from all his closest family members? Journal about your feelings related to writing about others, exploring the boundaries through various stories and relationships.

PRACTICE: Choose a potentially painful or embarrassing situation in your life and write about it freely. You don't have to share it with anyone, so include all the details, including your own pain and disappointment and struggle. Hold nothing back. Then set it aside and come back to it in a day or two. Upon rereading it, what would you have to omit or what permissions would you need to secure in order to tell the story as it is written? Can you do it? Is it time for this story to be told?

READ: "You Are in Paradise" by Zadie Smith from *The New Yorker,* June 14, 2004 Issue, about the author's trip to Tonga with a boyfriend, and "Shooting Dad" by Sarah Vowell in *Take the Cannoli: Stories From the New World,* 2000, Simon and Schuster, about the author's relationship with her father.

Would you have written about people in your life the way these writers did? In the first essay, "You Are in Paradise," Smith was able to leave the man unnamed, but Vowell writes about her dad. How did this affect what the authors were able to write? The title "Shooting Dad" sounds provocative, but the meaning is actually innocuous. Do you think the author intended the initial misunderstanding readers might have? How does that work to her advantage, particularly in writing about her father?

Chapter 8 • I'm Speaking: First-Person Voice

RESPOND: Do you have much experience with including *yourself* in your writing? Or were you trained in a style (academic, journalistic, business) that required you to keep yourself out of it? Or on the opposite extreme, do you write about ideas or events that are so personal you wonder whether anyone else would even care? How do you think first-person writing helps you connect with readers? As a reader, are you drawn to first-person writing?

PRACTICE: Find a story making headlines this week that you can relate to personally. Now, transform that news item into a personal essay by writing yourself into the story, offering your own opinions, experiences, and perspectives. How does the story change when the writer writes as a person? What was difficult about injecting yourself into the story?

READ: "Magical Dinners" by Chang-Rae Lee in *The New Yorker,* November 22, 2010 Issue, about one of the author's family's first American Thanksgivings, and "Nicki Minaj, Always in Control" by Roxanne Gay in *The New York Times,* October 16, 2017, a review of Minaj's new album. In these essays, the authors employ the first-person narrative technique, but with different results.

How did each author use the first person in service of the essay? Does either seem narcissistic, as we talked about in Chapter 8? How would the essays be different if the first person were removed entirely? Would either essay feel less "true" if it were told from a third-person point of view?

Chapter 9 • Finding the Funny

RESPOND: On a scale of 1 to 10, how funny do you think you are? Take some time to journal about your sense of humor. How would you describe it? What kinds of humor do you most enjoy listening to, reading, or watching? Do other people think of you as funny? Describe the last time you really burst out laughing. What was so funny? Now, on a scale of 1 to 10, how important is it to you to be able to write funny? Do you feel that a writer can learn humor? Of the techniques described in Chapter 9, which ones do you already employ?

PRACTICE: Quickly write down the specific sequence of events from the last meal you ate with someone else. Now, using some of the techniques outlined in Chapter 9, try to tell this same story humorously. Stick to the realm of actual events, but remember that techniques like exaggeration, understatement, and juxtaposition of opposites may stretch the truth a bit.

READ: "Three by Sedaris: The Youth in Asia, Jesus Shaves, and Giant Dreams, Midget Abilities" by David Sedaris from *Esquire*, January 29, 2007, and "The Real Mad Men" by Dave Berry, an excerpt from his book *Live Right and Find Happiness,* available for free on his website.

Did you think these essays were funny? Why or why not? Which of the techniques described in Chapter 9 did the writers employ? Did they work? If you didn't think these essays were funny, what other techniques do you think could have been used to make them funnier?

Chapter 10 • When It All Falls Apart

RESPOND: How aware are you of the sound of your own

voice? When did you first recognize it? When you think about editing or revision, do you ever worry that your voice will be stripped from your writing? What do you like best about your writing style? Can you identify specific elements that will help you accentuate your style rather than overwhelm the reader with it?

PRACTICE: Take ten minutes and write about something that happened to you over the past twenty-four hours. It might be pedestrian, normal, downright boring. Who cares? Just write it all out as much as you can remember. Now, using your word processing software (or your finger, if you wrote on paper), count the number of words. Your assignment is to cut the number of words in half without changing the meaning of the story. In fact, while you're cutting the words, also try to add more detail, more information. Prune the throwaway words (*the fact of the matter is* and *that* and *really*); get rid of the adjectives and adverbs and choose better nouns and verbs; try semicolons and get rid of some *and*s. You get the idea. When your word count is down to half, you're done.

READ: "Elements and Elegance: Fifty Years" by Willing Davidson for *The New Yorker,* April 15, 2009, about Strunk and White's *The Elements of Style,* which still has much to teach us as writers almost 60 years after it was first published, and "Revising your writing again? Blame the Modernists" by Craig Fehrman for *The Boston Globe,* June 30, 2013, which suggests that revision as we now think of it is a thoroughly modern practice.

How does the short essay about *The Elements of Style* employ many of the prescribed guidelines in the book it discusses? What can you learn from this essay and from *Elements* itself to help you revise your essays? In reading "Revising your writing again?" did you think the emphasis on revision is overblown? In what ways? Do you think some good writing can flow "from spontaneous and organic creative acts," as the Romantics believed?

Chapter 11 • Finishing

RESPOND: Take some time to consider and journal about your writing goals. If you already have clearly defined goals, consider whether they should be modified or clarified in line with your current desires. What surprises you about your goals? What has changed over time? Have any of your goals changed as a result of the work you have done or things you have learned in this book?

PRACTICE: Using the websites listed in Appendix C; publications you already are familiar with; portfolio webpages of other authors; or just good, old-fashioned Internet searches, come up with a list of 25-30 possible magazines, websites, or journals where you could send your work. Create a simple spreadsheet or some other organizing method to gather your information (back in the day, many of us used index cards to keep track of our submissions). What information will you need later when you're ready to submit your work? Capture it as you research so you can easily access it later when it's time to send.

READ: "Rebecca Solnit: 'The essay is powerful again. We're in a golden age'" in *The Guardian*, August 27, 2017, and "Are Essays Still Viable in the 21st Century?" by Patrick Madden for *The Huffington Post*, May 25, 2011. In both pieces, Solnit and Madden make the case that essays still belong in the larger world of publishing.

How do these essays make you feel about the prospect of writing and possibly publishing essays? Do the demands of "the market" play into your eagerness or hesitation to write in this form? Why does Solnit believe we need essays now more than ever? What aspects of essays does Madden argue are most relevant today?

Chapter 12 • Writing What Matters

RESPOND: What matters to you? Make a list of issues that are important to you. How could you add your voice to the conversation? Who else is talking about these issues in a meaningful way: both those you agree with and those you disagree with? What are the chances of becoming *persona non grata* among your closest friends and family if you write about these issues in a way that reflects not only your opinions but also your deepest questions? Do those around you tend to agree with you on these issues? Or disagree with you? Why do think that is?

PRACTICE: Choose a topic from a local or national newspaper and write a response as if you were writing an op-ed essay. Be precise in your writing by using shared language and writing in the context that's already been established by the original article and others like it. Think about standing by your words even as you write them. Do your tone, language, and meaning reflect how you would present yourself if you were speaking to someone in person? Would you be willing and able to further explain and explore your position if questioned?

READ: "The Future Needs Us" by Rebecca Solnit from *Tom's Dispatch*, December 22, 2013, and *Notes of a Native Son* by James Baldwin, Beacon Press, November 20, 2012, two essays that express the authors' passions about topics that are meaningful to their identity and work.

How do Solnit and Baldwin make their words matter in these essays? In what way does each author bear witness to a generation about what is happening in the world and what is at stake?

Appendix B:
Peer Review & Critique Guidelines

As you practice techniques and write essays, don't overlook or underestimate the importance of receiving feedback on your work.

But first, an acknowledgement. It's true we've all been disappointed or even paralyzed by a stinging critique too early in the process. Sometimes, we've received conflicting advice from two different readers. And occasionally, we just disagree with the opinions of others but feel forced to make changes we don't want to make.

This guide won't necessarily make that all go away. But what I hope to do is give you some strategies for getting (and giving) better feedback on your (and others') essays.

Ask For What You Need

Borrowing from the National Writing Project's Guidelines for Response Groups, let's think about giving and receiving feedback on three levels. Rather than handing your writing off blindly for a critique or peer review, instead, ask for what you want or need at this stage of your writing. Do you want the reader to admire, inquire, and/or perspire?

ADMIRE: Feeling uncertain about the way the essay is coming together, or trying to find the aspect of your work that really resonates? Ask readers for only what they admire, inviting them to comment on what's working well in the essay.

Sure, it has some problems. It's still an early draft. Make it clear to your readers that you understand that; otherwise, the more detail-oriented among them might not be able to let go of those comma splices or changing points of view. But when you just need to know which parts are on the right track, ask for only what's going well, for what they *admire* in your essay.

INQUIRE: When your draft is a little further along, or maybe you're feeling good about the work, invite readers to address just one or two overarching concerns they see. Of course they should also comment on what's working well. No one should ever turn down a chance to be admired. But when you're getting closer to "feeling" finished, having a reader inquire about a specific issue will help with what otherwise might be a blind spot for you.

PERSPIRE: Finally, before you send your work to a publication, invite a trusted reader, who also happens to know about grammar and punctuation, to go all out on your essay. Sure, they can tell you what's working, but more than that, you want to know anything that's not working. A trusted reader is key here, because now is not the time for tiptoeing around any major issues. You need someone who's willing to do the necessary hard work, to sweat it out with you. You're about to send this to an editor, and you'll want to put your best work out there every time.

Higher and Lower Order Concerns

Beyond giving yourself permission to ask for the level of feedback you want, it's also important for you—and any potential peer reviewers—to have a good sense of what issues to address and when. (You can include a brief explanation of the following along with any potential requests for review.)

The writing process includes two levels of concerns: higher order concerns and lower order concerns.

Higher order concerns address larger, "big picture" issues of the work as a whole—things like thesis, purpose, structure, and development. Working towards a well-written essay means strengthening the work in these areas first.

After the higher order concerns are addressed, writers can work more at the paragraph, sentence, and word level, and other lower order concerns: grammar, punctuation, usage, word choice, spelling, etc.

Don't let the words *higher* and *lower* imply too much a sense of greater and lesser importance here. Both levels matter to your writing, and problems in either can spell trouble. Generally, higher and lower refer to the order of priority in which these levels are addressed. First, address the big picture issues, then the lower order concerns, since there's no need to labor over a comma in the introduction if the whole thing needs to be written with a different focus anyway. But for many writers, the writing process—from drafting to revision—will move back and forth between the two.

So, within the "admire, inquire, perspire" framework we talked about above, you may want to ask for admiration or inquiry mostly about higher order concerns. When it comes time to perspire, however, both higher and lower order concerns should be on the table.

Additional Guidelines for Group Critique Sessions

If you're forming a writing critique group, you might consider these additional guidelines as a format for your meeting.

Before You Meet

The person whose work is being evaluated should send a copy to each participant a few days before the meeting and tell the readers what they are looking for: admire, inquire, or perspire? And higher order concerns, lower order concerns, or both?

Each participant should read each review piece ahead of time and make notes about the work on the printed copy so the writer can go back and review them later.

The goal is to provide insight that the author can't discern on her own. Comment on what aspects you really like and why, and how the piece affects you as a reader. Be specific. Unless the author has asked for it, remember not to focus on grammar or spelling.

During the Critique Group

The writer whose work is being evaluated will read a short excerpt (250-300 words) aloud to get everyone engaged with the piece. This will be extremely scary for some, but it also helps us practice hearing our work the way others hear it.

After the writer reads the excerpt, she should remain silent through the comments and responses—a response sometimes referred to as "wearing the cone of silence." (I've even seen groups mime the action of placing a cone over oneself as each member takes a turn at being critiqued—though maybe your group would prefer to don a silent superhero cloak!) No matter how much she wants to explain or agree or clarify, the writer should just receive what's expressed. After each reviewer has offered comments, the writer should simply say, "Thank you." When the critique session has ended, the writer can send an email to ask for clarification, but for now, she should just listen.

Each reviewer should share a few of their more noteworthy comments aloud for the whole group to hear. When speaking to the writer, keep in mind a few guidelines to help ease the sting that criticism often brings:

• Comment on both positive and negative aspects of the work, even if the writer has asked for feedback that goes beyond Admiration.

• Begin suggestions and observations with "I notice" instead of "you always" or other phrases that might make the writer feel on the spot.

• Refer to the writer as "the writer" or the narrator as "the narrator" rather than "you."

• After everyone has had a chance to share a few comments, give the writer the printed version of each critique and move on to the next essay for review.

Having your work reviewed and critiqued can be painful. Plan on feeling a little sting even if it's not your first critique and even if the majority of the comments are positive. You may find it difficult not to respond to the comments during the critique session, but taking that option off the table will actually put less pressure on you to respond in any particular way. The important thing to remember is you are the writer;

you can accept or reject any of the comments or suggestions. Try "in the margin" exercises when the solution isn't immediately obvious. At the very least, consider whether you can enhance or make clearer any of the sections that were commented upon. The reviewer likely has stumbled on a problem area, even if their suggestions for correcting it don't feel quite right to you.

Just like being a good writer, learning to be a good reviewer takes practice. Try to push beyond simple phrases like "I like it" and "It's good." Trust your instincts as a reader, and really work at providing helpful comments to your fellow writers. But also give yourself a break. If this process feels awkward and uncomfortable at first, you're likely not alone.

By the way, if you don't currently have a writing group, or if you've joined a group but would like to structure it so it's more helpful to members, visit tweetspeakpoetry.com and search for my article "How to Start, Join, & Make the Most of a Writing Group," originally published on June 5, 2015.

Appendix C: Where to Send Your Work

Rather than provide a specific list of publications that are currently accepting essay submissions (since that information could change in a New York minute), I'm going to provide a list of resources and websites that will help you search for publications that are accepting personal essays. With these few resources, you have dozens, if not hundreds, of potential publications to choose from.

Remember, always research. Review old copies of the publication you're submitting to for a better sense of what they publish. Also, don't rely on a guide or an aggregating post or website to have the submission guidelines correct. Do a search on the journal's or magazine's own website for what they want to receive and how you should send it.

Writer's Market. Both print and online versions are available at writersmarket.com. Before the Internet, the print version of *Writer's Market* was like the writer's bible and almost the only aggregated resource to find publishers and publications accepting submissions. It's still a useful resource for its nearly exhaustive information and regularly updated online version.

Submittable. This is an online submission platform that many journals and magazines use to streamline submissions. Some publications charge a fee to submit; others don't. You can also search for open calls for submissions, and track your previous submissions on Submittable. There's no cost for writers to join, though as I mentioned, you may have to pay for individual transactions. Find them at submittable.com.

Writers' Markets Facebook Page. This group is not related to the official *Writer's Market*, but it's loaded with all kinds of calls for submissions, especially for new or niche journals and magazines. The opportunities featured might not be for everyone, but it's at least worth checking out. Find them at facebook.com/groups/273421679453195/.

The Write Life. This is an online magazine that focuses on helping writers make money through writing. (And who doesn't want to do that?) Their post "19 Publications and Websites That Want Your Personal Essays" is particularly helpful. It can be found with a simple Internet search and offers a range of options for writers at all levels. Visit at thewritelife.com.

Every Writer. Writer and educator Richard Edwards publishes this online magazine, and among its many features, he offers a post of Top 50 Literary Magazines each year. Find it at everywritersresource.com/top50literarymagazines/. Some of these are major national publications, and others are smaller and regional.

Acknowledgements

I've written a book about "trying" to write, which is really all any of us can do. The love, support, and encouragement of others makes it an easier road.

To Laura Barkat, who first had the vision for this project as a workshop and then as a book, I'm forever grateful.

To Laura Brown, whose exceptional editing skills made this book so much better than it would have been otherwise, thank you for pushing and pulling in all the right places.

To Ann Kroeker, colleague, collaborator, and writing coach extraordinaire, your encouragement and friendship make the writing life so much more interesting and hysterical. You've helped me understand myself as an essayist, and you've helped me become a better one. Thank you.

To the participants of the fall 2015 essay workshop, thank you for the chance to workshop some of this material with you. In every comment and suggestion and critique, you served as the very best beta readers I could have asked for. And you wrote some mighty fine essays over those 12 weeks. It was an honor to learn alongside you.

To Scott Russell Sanders, Wendell Berry, Brian Doyle, Patrick Madden, Rebecca Solnit, Annie Dillard, E.B. White, Verlyn Klinkenborg, Ta-Nehisi Coates, Marilynne Robinson, and so many other essayists whose work I have pored over and admire, thank you for making this magpie form something we can all aspire to.

To Nicholas, Caleb, and Jacob, who got more than they bargained for when they ended up with a stepmom who writes, thank you for cheering me on and making space for me to write, even though it means giving up the best room in the house. I love you guys.

And to Steven, who knew exactly what it meant to have a wife who's a writer and married me anyway, thank you for every single way you support this calling and cheer me on as my most loyal fan. I love you more than words can express. (And for a writer, that's saying a lot.)

Credits & Sources

This book includes various references from or to the following companies, brands, and sources:

The New Yorker is a publication owned by Condé Nast; *The Atlantic* is a publication owned by The Atlantic Monthly Group LLC; Google Maps™ mapping service, Google Books™ service, Google™ search or search engine, and YouTube are all registered trademarks of Google LLC; Amazon is a registered trademark of Amazon.com, Inc.; Liquid-Text is an app owned and copyright protected by LiquidText Inc.; MindNode is an app owned and copyright protected by Ideas on Canvas GmbH, an independent software company based in Vienna, Austria; YMCA is a registered trademark of the National Council of Young Men's Christian Associations of the United States of America; Scotch is a trademark of 3M; NuStep is a registered trademark of NuStep, Inc.; IMDb is a registered trademark of IMDb.com; Facebook is a registered trademark of Facebook, Inc.; Netflix is a registered trademark of Netflix, Inc.; The Weather Channel is a registered trademark of The Weather Channel, Inc.; National Weather Service is a registered trademark of National Weather Service, National Oceanic and Atmospheric Administration, an agency of the United States Government; V8 is a registered trademark of CSC Brands, LP Campbell Finance 2 Corp; *Girl Meets God: On a Path to a Spiritual Life* was written by Lauren Winner and was published by Algonquin Books in 2002; *Banner Graphic* is a publication of Rust Communications, Inc.; *Miami Herald* is a publication of The McClatchy Company; *Yes, Please* by Amy Poehler was published by Dey Street Books in 2014; *Parks and Recreation* is a production of Deedle-Dee Productions, Fremulon, 3 Arts Entertainment and Universal Television; *Saturday Night Live* is a production of Broadway Video in association with SNL Studios; Chef Boyardee is a registered trademark of ConAgra Foods RDM, Inc.; Hostess Sno Balls is a registered trademark of Hostess Branks, LLC; Diet Pepsi is a registered trademark of Pepsico, Inc.; Pandora is a registered trademark of Pandora Media, Inc.; Trello is a registered trademark of Trello, Inc.; Band-Aid is a registered trademark of Johnson & Johnson; Red Bull is a registered trademark of Red Bull GMBH LLC; Air + Style is a registered trademark of Global Sports Limited; "Celebration" is a song released in 1980 by Kool & the Gang from their album *Celebrate!;* NFL is a registered trademark of the National Football League; "The MacNeil/Lehrer Report" was a feature of PBS NewsHour; the National Writing Project is a network of sites anchored at colleges and universities and serving teachers across disciplines and at all levels, early childhood through university.

Portions of chapters 2 and 11 were adapted from essays originally published at *Tweetspeak Poetry* under the following titles, "The Writing Life: The Writer's Delusion and Telling It Slant," "The Progression of a Writing Life Part 1: Play," "The Progression of a Writing Life Part 2: Risk," "The Progression of a Writing Life Part 3: Rejection," and "The Progression of a Writing Life Part 4: Strategy."

Endnotes

Let Me Introduce You

p. 9   "widest fattest most generous": Brian Doyle, "Playfulness: A Note" (Washington, D.C.: Welcome Table Press, 2010, accessed online on October 11, 2017).

p. 9   "There's nothing ordinary": Patrick Madden, "The Magpie Form" (Calvin College's 2012 Festival of Faith and Writing). Madden was loosely quoting an Alexander Smith essay, which he later anthologized in *Sublime Physick: Essays*. The original Smith quote is "The world is everywhere whispering essays, and one need only be the world's amanuensis."

p. 9   "The world is everywhere whispering": Alexander Smith, quoted during "The Magpie Form" (Calvin College's 2012 Festival of Faith and Writing).

p. 9   "The Magpie Form": This was a session about the essay offered at Calvin College's 2012 Festival of Faith and Writing.

p. 9   "recreating an experience": Patrick Madden, "The Magpie Form" (Calvin College's 2012 Festival of Faith and Writing).

p. 9   Essayists as "story-catchers": Brian Doyle, "The Magpie Form" (Calvin College's 2012 Festival of Faith and Writing).

p. 10   "I heard Scott Russell Sanders": Scott Russell Sanders gave the 2012 Kidwell Memorial Lecture at the Plainfield-Guilford Public Library in Plainfield, Indiana, on May 1, 2012.

p. 10   "miraculous power of language": Scott Russell Sanders, "Hunger for Books," *The Country of Language* (Minneapolis: Milkweed Editions, 1999), read by the author.

p. 10   "follow any question": Scott Russell Sanders, "Hunger for Books," *The Country of Language* (Minneapolis: Milkweed Editions, 1999), read by the author.

p. 10   "Michel de Montaigne": I gathered basic information about Michel de Montaigne from the Wikipedia page about his life. <https://en.wikipedia.org/wiki/Michel_de_Montaigne>

p. 10-11 "nothing he wrote about himself": Jane Kramer, "Me, Myself and I: What Made Michel de Montaigne the First Modern Man?" (*The New Yorker*, September 7, 2009, accessed online on October 11, 2017). <http://www.newyorker.com/magazine/2009/09/07/me-myself-and-i>

p. 11   "However you read them": Jane Kramer, "Me, Myself, and I: What Made Michel de Montaigne the First Modern Man?" (*The New Yorker*, September 7, 2009, accessed online on October 11, 2017). <http://www.newyorker.com/magazine/2009/09/07/me-myself-and-i>

p. 11   "has been largely hijacked and adulterated beyond recognition": Patrick Madden, "The Essayest American Essays 2016" (*Quotidiana*, undated, accessed online October 31, 2017). < http://cae.quotidiana.org/>

p. 11   "people don't want to read essays": Patrick Madden, "Are Essays Viable in the Twenty-First Century?" (*The Huffington Post*, May 25, 2011, accessed online October 11, 2017). <http://www.huffingtonpost.com/patrick-madden/are-essays-viable-in-the_b_518797.html>

p. 12   "2014 *The New York Times* Bookends article": Cheryl Strayed and Benjamin Moser, "Is This a Golden Age for Women Essayists?" (*The New York Times*, October 12, 2014, accessed online on October 11, 2017). <https://www.nytimes.com/2014/10/12/books/review/is-this-a-golden-age-for-women-essayists.html?_r=0>

p. 12   "*The New Yorker* declared the personal essay boom over": Jia Tolentino, "The Personal Essay Boom Is Over" (*The New Yorker*, May 18, 2017, accessed online on October 11, 2017). <http://www.newyorker.com/culture/jia-tolentino/the-personal-essay-boom-is-over>

p. 12   "powerful and compelling again": Rachel Cooke, "Rebecca Solnit: 'The essay is powerful again. We're in a golden age'" (*The Guardian*, August 27, 2017, accessed online on January 17, 2018).

p. 12   "as a person": Bill Roorbach, *Writing Life Stories: How to Make Memories into Memoirs, Ideas into Essays, and Life into*

Literature (Cincinnati: Writers Digest Books, 2008), p. 69.

Chapter 1

p. 14   "to be one of the people": Henry James, "The Art of Fiction" (*Longman's Magazine*, September 1884), accessed online June 10, 2019, via Washington State University website. <https://public.wsu.edu/~campbelld/amlit/artfiction.html>

p. 15   "story on WBUR's *Here and Now*": "The Risks And Rewards Of Hummingbird Rescue" (WBUR's *Here and Now*, broadcast on July 28, 2015, via WFYI 90.1, accessed online on October 30, 2017). <https://hereandnow.wbur.org/2015/07/28/hummingbird-rescue-masear>

p. 16   "one means of coping": Barbara M. Benedict, *Making the Modern Reader: Cultural Mediation in Early Modern Literary Anthologies* (Princeton: Princeton University Press, 1996), accessed online via A Commonplace Book on October 30, 2017). <http://3stages.org/quotes/cpb.html>

Chapter 2

p. 20   "what we can do": Bill Roorbach, *Writing Life Stories: How to Make Memories into Memoirs, Ideas into Essays, and Life into Literature* (Cincinnati: Writers Digest Books, 2008), p. 26-27.

p. 20   "Memory has its own story to tell": Tobias Wolff on the acknowledgements page of *This Boy's Life: A Memoir*.

p. 21   "perhapsing": Lisa Knopp, 'Perhapsing': The Use of Specu-
         lation in Creative Nonfiction" (*Brevity*, Issue 29, January
         2009, accessed online October 30, 2017). < https://www.
         creativenonfiction.org/brevity/craft/craft_knopp1_09.htm>

p. 24   "Tell all the truth but tell it slant": Emily Dickinson, *The
         Poems of Emily Dickinson: Reading Edition* (Boston: The
         Belknap Press of Harvard University Press, 1998, accessed
         online via Poetry Foundation October 30, 2017).

Chapter 3

p. 26   "My novels all begin" and "peel back the layers": Dani
         Shapiro, "On Inquiry" (DaniShapiro.com, July 10, 2015,
         accessed online October 30, 2017).
         <http://danishapiro.com/on-inquiry/>

p. 26   "Too often students think": Scott Russell Sanders inter-
         viewed by Robert L. Root (*The Fourth Genre*, Spring 1999,
         accessed online October 30, 2017). < http://www.scott
         russellsanders.com/about/fourthgenreint.html>

p. 27   "There was so much to find": Wil S. Hylton, "The Un-
         breakable Laura Hillenbrand" (*The New York Times*,
         December 18, 2014, accessed online October 30, 2017).
         < https://www.nytimes.com/2014/12/21/magazine/
         the-unbreakable-laura-hillenbrand.html>

Chapter 4

p. 32   "critical mass of ideas": Scott Russell Sanders interviewed
         by Robert L. Root (*The Fourth Genre*, Spring 1999, accessed
         online October 30, 2017). <http://www.scottrussell-
         sanders.com/about/fourthgenreint.html>

Chapter 5

p. 38   "only the biggest landmarks": Gail Carson Levine, *Writing
         Magic: Creating Stories that Fly* (New York: Harper, 2006),
         p. 107.

p. 38   "Don't tell me the moon": Anton Chekhov, no specific
         attribution, found via Quote Investigator, accessed March
         7, 2018. < https://quoteinvestigator.com/2013/07/30/
         moon-glint/>

p. 38   "Don't tell me the old lady": Mark Twain, no specific attri-
         bution, found via BrainyQuote, accessed March 7, 2018.
         < https://www.brainyquote.com/quotes/mark_twain_
         133972>

p. 38   "Show the readers everything": Ernest Hemingway,
         no specific attribution, found via Goodreads, accessed
         March 7, 2018. < https://www.goodreads.com/quotes/
         381362-show-the-readers-everything-tell-them-nothing>

p. 39   "clinically dissect all showing and telling": Alice LaPlante,
         The Making of a Story (New York: WW Norton and Com-

pany, 2007), p. 222.

p. 39   "because good telling is difficult": Alice LaPlante,
           The Making of a Story (New York: WW Norton and
           Company, 2007), p. 216.

Chapter 6

p. 43   "As is often the case, Robert was there": This name has
           been changed to preserve the privacy of the subject.

p. 44   "play persistently with language": Namrata Poddar, "Is
           'Show Don't Tell' a Universal Truth or a Colonial Relic?"
           (*Literary Hub,* September 20, 2016, accessed online March 6,
           2018). <https://lithub.com/is-show-dont-tell-a-universal-
           truth-or-a-colonial-relic/>

p. 45   "No human work can become whole by including
           everything": Wendell Berry, *Imagination in Place* (Berkeley:
           Counterpoint, 2010), p. 3.

p. 45   "at least call farming tools": Wendell Berry, *Imagination in
           Place* (Berkeley: Counterpoint, 2010), p. 13.

p. 45   "get sophisticated about carnal writing": Mary Karr,
           The Art of Memoir (New York, Harper, 2015), p. 72.

p. 46   "Writers very often need to be away from a place": Annie
           Dillard, quoted by Diana Saverin in "The Thoreau of the
           Suburbs" (*The Atlantic*, February 5, 2015, accessed online

October 30, 2017). <http://www.theatlantic.com/features/archive/2015/02/the-thoreau-of-the-suburbs/385128/>

p. 46   "be faithful at once": Scott Russell Sanders, "Letter to a Reader," *Earth Works: Selected Essays* (Bloomington: Indiana University Press, 2012), p. 153.

Chapter 7

p. 51   "found the essay so helpful" and "left the essay in my drawer": Scott Russell Sanders, in an interview for *Quotidiana* (*Quotidiana*, March 2, 2006, accessed online October 31, 2017). <http://interviews.quotidiana.org/pdfs/sanders.pdf>

p. 51   "How much can we show": Joy Castro, "Family Trouble: Respect and Responsibility in the Craft of Memoir" (*Signature,* October 1, 2013, accessed online October 31, 2017). <http://www.signature-reads.com/2013/10/family-trouble-respect-and-responsibility-in-the-craft-of-memoir/>

p. 52   "You own everything that happened to you": Anne Lamott (Twitter, April 23, 2012, accessed online October 31, 2017). <https://twitter.com/annelamott/status/194580559962439681>

p. 52   "As scary as possible judgment or rejection": Sue Williams Silverman, "The Courage to Write and Publish Your Story:

Five Reasons Why it's Important to Write Memoir | Essay
— Sue William Silverman" (*Numero Cinquo*, Vol. II, No. 9,
September 2011, accessed online October 31, 2017).
<http://numerocinqmagazine.com/2011/09/24/
the-courage-to-write-and-publish-your-story-five-reasons-
why-its-important-to-write-memoir-by-sue-william-
silverman/>

p. 52   "If you … treat people … with complexity": Kim Barnes,
           Fourth Genre interview, quoted by Silverman Sue Williams
           Silverman, "The Courage to Write and Publish Your Story:
           Five Reasons Why it's Important to Write Memoir | Essay
           — Sue William Silverman" (*Numero Cinquo*, Vol. II, No. 9,
           September 2011, accessed online October 31, 2017).
           <http://numerocinqmagazine.com/2011/09/24/
           the-courage-to-write-and-publish-your-story-five-reasons-
           why-its-important-to-write-memoir-by-sue-william-
           silverman/>

p. 53   "When I write I find out things": Rebecca Solnit, inter-
           viewed by Walter Biggins (Bookslut, June 2013, accessed
           online October 31, 2017). <http://www.bookslut.com/
           features/2013_06_020127.php>

p. 53   "In *Writing Life Stories*, Bill Roorbach not only": Bill
           Roorbach, *Writing Life Stories: How to Make Memories into
           Memoirs, Ideas into Essays, and Life into Literature* (Cincinnati:
           Writers Digest Books, 2008).

p. 54   "I once heard author Lauren Winner": Lauren Winner interviewed by Darlene Meyering at the 2006 Festival of Faith and Writing at Calvin College in Grand Rapids, Mich.

Chapter 8

p. 57   "Selves, as it turns out, are awfully complicated": Bill Roorbach, *Writing Life Stories: How to Make Memories into Memoirs, Ideas into Essays, and Life into Literature* (Cincinnati: Writers Digest Books, 2008), p. 131.

p. 57   "What we meet on the page": Scott Russell Sanders, "The Singular First Person," *Earth Works: Selected Essays* (Bloomington: Indiana University Press, 2012), p. 10.

p. 58   "proficient use of the language": William Strunk Jr. and E.B. White, *The Elements of Style* (New York: MacMillan Publishing Co., 1979), p. 70

p. 58   "Style' shouldn't linger in your awareness": Verlyn Klinkenborg, *A Few Short Sentences about Writing* (New York: Vintage Books, 2013), p. 85.

p. 59   "sustained by the childish belief": E.B. White, *Essays of E.B. White* (New York: Harper Perennial Modern Classics, 2016), p. ix.

p. 59   "will matter to everyone": Donna Talarico, "The Unslanted Truth: a Conversation With Four Editors of Today's Premier Creative Nonfiction Literary Magazines" interview with Courtney Leigh (*The Review Review*, undated, accessed online October 31, 2017). < http://www.thereviewreview.net/publishing-tips/unslanted-truth-conversation-four-editors-to>

p. 60   "I choose to write about my experience not because it is mine": Scott Russell Sanders, "The Singular First Person," *Earth Works: Selected Essays* (Bloomington: Indiana University Press, 2012), p. 8.

p. 60   "'A House for Birds' wasn't quite there": Charity Singleton Craig, "A House for Birds" (*The Curator Magazine*, December 8, 2014, accessed online October 31, 2017). <http://www.curatormagazine.com/charity-singleton/a-house-for-birds/>

p. 61   "what somebody's telling you": John Covach, interviewed by Adrienne LaFrance, "Me, Myself, and Authenticity" (*The Atlantic*, February 25, 2015, accessed online October 31, 2017). <https://www.theatlantic.com/technology/archive/2015/02/the-unassuming-power-of-pronouns/385979/>

Chapter 9

p. 62   "what happens to Cousin Ron": Name and details changed to preserve privacy.

p. 64   "Humor can be dissected": This quote is attributed to E.B. and Katharine S. White, "The Preaching Humorist" (*The Saturday Review of Literature,* October 18, 1941, accessed

online at Quote Investigator on October 11, 2017).
<https://quoteinvestigator.com/2014/10/14/frog/>

p. 65   "Humor is rigorous stuff": Siobhan Adcock, "Why Every
Writer Should Take a Humor Writing Class" (*The Huffington
Post*, November 12, 2014, accessed online on October 11,
2017). <http://www.huffingtonpost.com/siobhan-
adcock/why-every-writer-should-t_b_5811562.html>

p. 66   "director Harold Ramis says": Scott Simon, interview with
Harold Ramis, "Comedy Writing: How To Be Funny"
(NPR's Weekend Edition Saturday, August 1, 2009,
transcript accessed online on October 11, 2017).
<http://www.npr.org/templates/story/story.php?
storyId=111456667>

p. 67   "List two expected items": Teddy Wayne, "Dissecting a
Frog: How to Write a Humor Piece" (*The New York Times*,
February 3, 2014, accessed online on October 11, 2017).
<https://opinionator.blogs.nytimes.com/2014/02/03/
dissecting-a-frog-how-to-write-a-humor-piece/?_r=0>

Chapter 10

p. 70   "a quick burst of dopamine": Christopher Bergland,
"The Neurochemicals of Happiness" (*Psychology Today*,
November 29, 2012, accessed online March 7, 2018).
<https://www.psychologytoday.com/blog/the-athletes-
way/201211/the-neurochemicals-happiness>

p. 70   "I'm done, I'm done": paraphrase of the line, "I'm in love,
         I'm in love, and I don't care who knows it." From *Elf*
         (New Line Cinema, Director: Jon Favreau, Writer: David
         Berenbaum, 2003). <https://www.youtube.com/watch?v=
         Pd0VBm8gU5o>

p. 71   "omit needless words": William Strunk Jr. and E.B. White,
         The Elements of Style (New York: MacMillan Publishing Co.,
         1979), p. 23.

p. 71   "All writing is revision": Verlyn Klinkenborg, *A Few Short
         Sentences about Writing* (New York: Vintage Books, 2013),
         p. 85.

p. 71   "raises the odds that a writer": Alice LaPlante, *The Making
         of a Story* (New York: WW Norton and Company, 2007),
         p. 544.

p. 71   "Murder [our] darlings": Sir Arthur Quiller-Couch, 1913-
         1914 Cambridge lectures "On the Art of Writing."
         < http://www.bartleby.com/190/>

p. 75   "exercise-based revision": Alice LaPlante, *The Making of a
         Story*, p. 551.

p. 76   "a metaphorical stick of dynamite": Alice LaPlante,
         The Making of a Story, p. 552.

Chapter 11

p. 77   "I hate the fact I nailed it in practice": Shaun White, interviewed by ESPN, "Shaun White: 'I'm disappointed'" (ESPN, February 12, 2014, accessed online October 31, 2017). <http://espn.go.com/olympics/winter/2014/snowboarding/story/_/id/10438109/2014-sochi-olympics-shaun-white-finishes-4th-halfpipe-iouri-podladtchikov-wins-gold>

p. 78   "Honestly, it's one of the most challenging": Shaun White, quoted in Shawn Smith's, "Shaun White wins USA's 100th all-time Winter Olympic gold medal" (NBCOlympics.com, February 13, 2018, accessed online March 9, 2018). <https://www.nbcolympics.com/news/shaun-white-wins-usas-100th-all-time-winter-olympic-gold-medal>

p. 78   "selfish jerk": Elizabeth Weil, "The Flying Tomato Would Rather You Not Call Him That Anymore" (*The New York Times Magazine*, January 12, 2014, accessed online October 31, 2017). <http://www.nytimes.com/2014/01/12/magazine/the-flying-tomato-would-rather-you-not-call-him-that-anymore.html?_r=0>

p. 81   "The whole strategizing thing is what does it for me," Shaun White interviewed by Elizabeth Weil, "The Flying Tomato Would Rather You Not Call Him That Anymore" (The New York Times Magazine, January 12, 2014, accessed online October 31, 2017). <http://www.ny times.com/2014/01/12/magazine/the-flying-tomato-

would-rather-you-not-call-him-that-anymore.html?_r=0>

p. 83   "understanding that our work": Louise DeSalvo, *The Art of Slow Writing: Reflections on Time, Craft, and Creativity* (New York: St. Martin's Grififn, 2014), p. 276.

Chapter 12

p. 85   "A proper argument takes intellectual vigor": Hanna Rosin "The Tricks People Use to Avoid Debate" (*The Atlantic*, July/August 2015, accessed online October 31, 2017). <http://www.theatlantic.com/magazine/archive/2015/07/there-will-be-no-debate/395252/>

p. 86   "My impression is that we have seen": Wendell Berry, "Standing by Words," *Standing by Words* (Berkeley: Counterpoint, 1983), Kindle edition.

p. 87   "tension either between": Wendell Berry, "Standing by Words," *Standing by Words* (Berkeley: Counterpoint, 1983), Kindle edition.

p. 88   "must believe it, be accountable for it, be willing to act on it": Wendell Berry, "Standing by Words," *Standing by Words* (Berkeley: Counterpoint, 1983), Kindle edition.

p. 89   "write in order to win sympathy": Scott Russell Sanders interviewed by Robert L. Root (*The Fourth Genre*, Spring 1999, accessed online October 30, 2017). <http://www.scottrussellsanders.com/about/fourthgenreint.html>

p. 89   "always felt uncomfortable": Gregory Cowles, "Oliver
         Sacks, Neurologist Who Wrote about the Brain's Quirks,
         Dies at 82" (*The New York Times*, August 30, 2015, accessed
         online October 31, 2017).
         <http://www.nytimes.com/2015/08/31/science/
         oliver-sacks-dies-at-82-neurologist-and-author-
         explored-the-brains-quirks.html>

p. 89   "dramatis persona": an actor in a play

p. 89   "I've tried to imagine what it was like": Oliver Sacks in a
         1989 interview with Joanna Simon for The MacNeil/
         Lehrer Report of PBS NewsHour, quoted by Gregory
         Cowles, "Oliver Sacks, Neurologist Who Wrote about the
         Brain's Quirks, Dies at 82" (*The New York Times*,
         August 30, 2015, accessed online October 31, 2017).

p. 90   "Being a writer is part of a noble tradition": Anne Lamott,
         Bird by Bird (New York: Anchor Books, 1994), p. 235.

Epilogue

p. 91   "I didn't stop and look around": Neil Gaiman, "Make
         Good Art" (commencement speech to Philadelphia's
         University of the Arts, May 2012, accessed online at
         YouTube October 31, 2017). <https://www.youtube.
         com/watch?v=ikAb-NYkseI>

p. 92   "If we see our writing life": *The Art of Slow Writing:
         Reflections on Time, Craft, and Creativity* (New York:
         St. Martin's Grififn, 2014), p. 276.

Also from T. S. Poetry Press

Rumors of Water: Thoughts on Creativity & Writing, by L.L. Barkat (Twice named a Best Book of 2011)

A few brave writers pull back the curtain to show us their creative process. Annie Dillard did this. So did Hemingway. Now L.L. Barkat has given us a thoroughly modern analysis of writing. Practical, yes, but also a gentle uncovering of the art of being a writer.

– Gordon Atkinson, Editor at Laity Lodge

How to Write a Poem: Based on the Billy Collins Poem "Introduction to Poetry," by Tania Runyan

How to Write a Poem uses images like the buzz, the switch, the wave—from the Billy Collins poem "Introduction to Poetry"—to guide writers into new ways of writing poems. Excellent teaching tool. Anthology and prompts included.

On Being a Writer: 12 Simple Habits for a Writing Life That Lasts, by Ann Kroeker & Charity Singleton Craig

A genial marriage of practice and theory. For writers new and seasoned. This book is a winner.

—Philip Gulley, author of *Front Porch Tales*

T. S. Poetry Press titles are available online in e-book and print editions. Print editions also available through Ingram.

tspoetry.com

Printed by Amazon Italia Logistica S.r.l.
Torrazza Piemonte (TO), Italy

MINIMALISM FOR FAMILIES: MINDFUL, PRACTICAL WAYS TO DECLUTTER YOUR LIFE

Why Less Is More for Your Family
and How to Simply Create
A Happy, Calm and Chaos-Free
Home Environment

GRACE STOCKHOLM

TABLE OF CONTENTS

(Before you continue to read, make sure
to download your complimentary bonus)

ACTIVITIES FOR A MINIMALIST FAMILY

Fun Activities to Declutter Your Home and Heart

What's in store with this practical bonus:

- The complete list of minimalism activities for your family;
- Practical ways to enjoy these activities at home;
- Advice on how to go beyond the activities and become a true minimalist.

Minimalism is a great choice for you and your family regardless of your past experiences.

Click the link below to get your free activities ideas:

http://gracestockholm.net/activities-of-a-minimalist-family

INTRODUCTION:

THE WONDERFUL WORLD OF MINIMALISM

Family life can be both rewarding and challenging. Before having a family of your own, you might have already heard a lot of stories about living with your own family—both the good sides and the challenging sides. Although family life comes with quite a few challenges, one of the most frustrating is the feeling like there is just no space left for you. No matter how big your home is, things will pile up, you will find clutter everywhere you look and soon, this will start taking a toll on your mind, your soul, and even your health. If you don't do anything to change this, things will only get worse. And if you find yourself at a point where you just want to want to be left alone, leave your home, and everything else behind, this is probably because your life right now is way too complicated.

So what should you do about it?

Instead of leaving everything else behind—especially your family—you should consider minimalism. This is a wonderful way to live your life to the fullest by making things simpler. Through minimalism, you will realize that family life doesn't have to be a challenge. Instead, it is a blessing that you can be grateful for each day. When you become a minimalist, you will learn how to care more about the people and the environment around you instead of the material things that surround

1

you. Minimalism involves getting rid of extra things like clothes, furniture, toys, appliances, and any other items that you don't need. These are the items that contribute to the clutter you feel in your mind and soul. And when you work to keep your home and your environment free of this clutter, you can focus more on what really matters...spending quality time with your family in a relaxed and safe space.

These days, a lot of families are having a hard time making ends meet. We hear about stories of families who feel sad, worried, and frustrated because they cannot afford the things that they want, yet they buy those things anyway. Eventually, these families end up being buried in debts just because they couldn't resist the call of consumerism. Does this sound familiar to you?

It's time to make a change.

You may have already heard the old, well-known phrase: "less is more." Simple as this saying may seem, it is what minimalists live by to make their life better. Unfortunately, in today's modern world, people may see those who have less as weak, poor, and undesirable. Unless you have a huge house filled with expensive things, you won't belong to certain elite groups—the ones that a lot of people yearn to be a part of. But this isn't what family life should be about. In fact, a lot of families who seem to be doing well because they own a lot of stuff aren't really happy.

When it comes to happiness and wealth, these two things are often filled with contradictions. Those who don't have wealth feel unhappy because they cannot afford material things. On the other hand, those who have more money than they know what to do with aren't happy either because they are too busy trying to earn more just so they can sustain the lifestyles they have built for themselves. Both look at each other thinking, "they must be happy" while yearning for things that they don't have.

Through hard work and dedication, some of those "poor people" manage to bring their families out of poverty. When this happens, they would, of course, feel happier. But this happiness doesn't last long. Along with wealth and material things come more complicated situations, thus, increasing their likelihood of encountering day-to-day frustrations. For instance, if you as a parent would purchase an expensive gadget for your child for the first time—because you can afford it now—how would you feel if your child lost or broke that gadget? Since your child isn't used to such a device, they wouldn't know how to care for it or keep it safe. And when you find out what happened, you'd probably feel upset because you spent so much money on it. At that moment, would you have time to think about what your child might be feeling?

When your child realizes that they lost or broke the expensive gadget given to them, they would feel anxious about it. Still, because you have a good relationship, your child gathers the courage to come clean. And you react by getting angry and scolding them for losing or breaking something so expensive. In such a situation, what do you think happens to your relationship? Does it become stronger or does it get damaged? Obviously, it's the latter.

Although you might try to make your child feel better by talking to them after you've cooled down, the damage has already been done. You've already said hurtful things all because of a material thing. Yes, it's expensive. Yes, you worked hard to buy that thing for your child. And yes, your child should learn how to care for their things. But are these things more important than your relationship with your child? Or even your parent, your sibling or your spouse?

No, they aren't.

This is one of the many situations that you can avoid through minimalism. Whether you already own a lot of material things ("a lot" is subjective, of course, and only you know what feel a lot to you) or you have come into a lot of wealth and you're thinking about what to do with it, minimalism can help improve your life. Through minimalism, you can improve your family's life by learning how to free yourself from the trap of spending more than you can afford, living in a home or environment that is bigger than you and your family need, and putting material things over your health, your life, and the people who matter most to you. Through minimalism, you will learn how to appreciate and feel grateful for what truly matters.

Clutter can take many forms from things, tasks, fears, discontent, and more. And the more clutter you have in your life, the more dissatisfied and unhappy you will be. If you have a family, it's an especially unhealthy way to live life. Minimalism isn't just for those who live alone; families need minimalism too. This will help you and your family let go of everything that is causing ill feelings, stress, and negativity. Through everything you will learn in this book, you will be able to lead your family into a happier, more fulfilling life.

It's time to put an end to the chaos. Stop trying to do everything. Stop trying to spend more than you have. Stop collecting things that you don't need. Instead, start being more grateful. Start being more organized. Start learning how to nurture your family. Start learning how to become a minimalist.

Minimalists enjoy life to the fullest because they experience life to the fullest. They don't try to find happiness in material things. In fact, the less they have, the more they rely on their relationships and their own actions to be happy and stay happy. Minimalists encourage their whole family to adopt the same lifestyle so that they can spend more quality time together, feel satisfied living in a home that they can afford, and create genuine bonds that people who focus on material things can only dream about. When you learn how to become a minimalist and you teach it to your family, you can enjoy benefits like:

- Being able to breathe in your environment
- Experiencing less stress
- Being able to focus on things that are important in life
- Having more time to spend with each other
- Finding it easier to travel together even on a whim

- Feeling happier even at the smallest triumphs
- ... and so much more!

Minimalism isn't just an idea or a trend that goes away after some time. This is one concept that has been scientifically tested and proven to be healthy for the mind and body. Minimalism works for individuals, couples, and families, giving the same incredible results. And all you have to do is give it a try.

By the end of this book, you will have a rich and comprehensive understanding of what minimalism is all about and how it can help you and your whole family declutter from the life you have now so that you can achieve the life you want. Within the pages of this book, you will learn how to adapt the minimalist posture by cleaning your home, your environment, and your workspace to gain back your physical and mental health so you can experience life to the fullest.

As a promise to you, this book will help you learn how to make better choices for yourself and your family. Throughout the book, you will learn proven exercises and practices that minimalists all over the world have been using to live happier lives and have closer bonds with their families. Whether you are a mom, a dad, a teenager, a young adult or even a child, minimalism will change your life for the better.

Although there are so many books on minimalism out there that you could have chosen, the fact is, most of them won't give you what you need. Fortunately, you chose this book that is completely dedicated to families and to people who are planning to start their own families. Here, you will learn several actionable tips, practical advice, and achievable exercises that you can do to learn about and apply minimalism to your life directly. This book goes beyond theory and guides you to becoming a true minimalist for yourself and your family.

While decluttering your life won't be an easy task, you can do it when you have the right tools and information. It's time to start breaking your bad habits until you get minimalism right. The good news is, once you start using the practical tips and strategies in this book, you will start feeling and seeing the benefits of minimalism. That is when you will realize that it is truly a better way to live. With that being said... are you ready to live a better life with less?

CHAPTER 1:

A DECLUTTERED INTRODUCTION TO MINIMALISM

Becoming a minimalist teaches you to focus on and appreciate the more important things in life. But it's also an excellent weapon against all of the sales, services, and products that you would normally give into even though you can't really afford them or don't really need them. And the best part about minimalism is that the longer you practice it, the more you will realize how it is changing your life for the better. Soon, you will come to realize that you don't need all of the things that surround your home to feel unique, content, safe, and happy.

Of course, I don't mean that you should get rid of everything you own right away. You should still keep some of the most fundamental items that you own to make your life comfortable while allowing you to enjoy the feeling of owning material possessions. At some level, you should protect your own interests so you won't feel like you have given up too much too fast. To become a true minimalist, you should learn how to set your boundaries so you don't feel resentment or regret. Minimalism should be about happiness, positivity, and finding the good in letting go.

In this first chapter, I will be introducing the concept of minimalism to you. For you to understand what minimalism is all about and start applying it to your life, you should learn what minimalism is, a brief history of it, and what it involves. By learning what minimalism is, you will have a better idea of what you should expect and how you will transform your life into one that isn't cluttered by insignificant and unnecessary things. Also, understanding minimalism better will make you feel more inspired to start taking steps in the right direction for your own sake and for the sake of your family.

What Is Minimalism

These days, minimalism is a very popular word that carries a lot of weight. A lot of people want to become minimalists but once they discover what it really means, they hesitate because they can't let go of their material possessions or the other things that clutter their lives. Because of the recent interest in minimalism, countless books, documentaries, articles, podcasts, and more have been made about this subject. Unfortunately, a lot of them only scratch the surface of this simple way of life.

Minimalism is more than a modern-day fad. If you follow it correctly and you have pure intentions for practicing it, minimalism will provide significant benefits to your life. The simplest definition of minimalism is to intentionally get rid of or eliminate all the excess things in your life. That way, you can focus your time, love, and energy on the things that truly matter to you. Minimalism is a choice, it involves a lifestyle change, not just decluttering your home and cutting down on the material things that you own. Instead, minimalism involves taking a conscious look at everything you have, reflecting on what you really need, and working towards a life that you want to live.

When you adopt a minimalist mindset, you will intentionally prioritize the things in your life that you believe are essential. It involves letting go of the things you don't need, and the things that you don't consider important. This allows you to focus more on the right things while giving you a sense of freedom that's unlike anything you have ever experienced in your life. Minimalism can also be a tool to improve your life and free you from worry, guilt, fear, depression, and other negative feelings that come with having too much and wanting too much. Through minimalism, you can honestly say that you are free.

But let me clarify one important thing that a lot of people don't understand about minimalism. As a minimalist, I don't believe that there is anything wrong with owning and placing value on material possessions. But when you start giving too much meaning to those possessions that you start forsaking your personal growth, passion, health, and even your relationships because of those possessions, this is when they become a problem in your life. For instance, if you are focused too much on owning your dream house, you might end up spending too many hours at the office while your spouse and children are left to fend for themselves at home. You might end up with the home of your dreams but no family to share it with. Wouldn't this be a tragedy?

But if you can find contentment through minimalism, you won't keep looking for things that you don't have. Instead, you will focus on the blessings you *do* have, thus, being happier and more content with your life. You can still aspire for that dream house, but you will enjoy the journey. Simply put, minimalism helps you:

- Eliminate the things that don't add value to your life
- Spend more time experiencing things with those you love instead of spending more money on things that you don't really need
- Reduce or even eliminate financial worry from your life
- Go green
- Nurture your relationships (especially with your family) to make them stronger
- Feel happier because you feel less stressed

These are the most significant benefits minimalism can bring to your life. While you can become a true minimalist to appreciate your family more, you can also share this lifestyle with the members of your family so you can all experience all the wonderful things minimalism has to offer. Here are some examples of what minimalism may look like for the different members of your family:

- **For babies and toddlers**
  - You would only buy the bare essentials for your baby such as food, clothing, diapers, and the like. Of course, you should have enough clothing for your baby since babies are quite messy, especially when it comes to eating, peeing, drooling, pooping, and more.
  - As your baby grows into a toddler, you may need to buy more clothes. This depends on how active or how messy your toddler is. Just make sure that you have enough. Minimalism doesn't mean that you will deprive your children of the things they need to grow up happy and healthy.
  - While toddlers love to play with toys, you don't have to buy the most expensive ones, the latest releases or even excessive amounts of toys if you want to adopt minimalism. Again, just get enough toys to entertain your toddler. In fact, you can even rotate your toddler's toys by bringing out a few at a time and when they get bored, give them another set while storing the toys they're tired of. Then when they get bored with the current set, bring out the first set and see how they will react to it. Toddlers don't need a lot of toys. What they need is attention, love, and your presence to make them happy.
- **For children**
  - The older your children get, the easier it is to practice minimalism. You can buy fewer clothes and toys. You can also start teaching your child how to take care of their possessions so they last for a long time.
  - As a minimalist, you should also consider the activities you allow your child to engage in carefully. Don't push your child to have a schedule that's busier than yours. Instead, allow your child to choose what they want to do while

10

making sure that they have time to do everything while still having spare time to do things that they actually want to do.

- **For teenagers and young adults**
  - o If you started teaching your child how to live a minimalist lifestyle from the beginning, they will carry these habits until they grow into teenagers, young adults, and adults. Ultimately, though, you should allow your teenager or young adult to make their own decisions. If they want to continue practicing minimalism, guide them. If not, allow them to explore other lifestyles while still continuing with your own minimalist path.
  - o When your teenager starts college as a minimalist, they won't have to worry about moving to a different area, spending too much money on things, especially those they don't need, and having to bring all of their stuff everywhere they go since they don't own a lot of stuff to begin with.
- **For your parents**
  - o If you live with your parents or they live with you, minimalism can improve their lives too. They will have more freedom with their energy and time, thus, allowing them to bond with you and their grandchildren to make their golden years much happier.

Now that you understand what minimalism means, you should have a clearer picture of what it entails. As you can see, minimalism isn't just for adults or people who live alone. Even when you have a family, minimalism can be part of your life. In fact, it will be one of the best parts as it opens your world to freedom, stronger bonds, and discovering the unconditional love that exists between you and all the other members of your family.

The Key Ideas of Minimalism

Minimalism is a wonderful thing and recently, more and more people have come to realize this fact. In this modern world filled with pressure, stress, and clutter, minimalism is a refreshing change that can bring more to your life despite its nature of living with less. Unfortunately, there are a lot of myths and misconceptions about minimalism and this is the reason why a lot of people don't take the leap into this lifestyle. If you're one such person, learning the key ideas of minimalism may help you out. Now that you know more about minimalism and what's involved in it, let's go through the fundamental ideas behind it to clarify the key tenets of minimalism for a profound understanding.

1. **Minimalism isn't just about getting rid of everything that you own**

   Although getting rid of your material things is a huge part of minimalism, you shouldn't focus only on these unnecessary things that you are removing from your life. Instead, you should focus more on the things that you gain because of your willingness to let go of the things that don't add value to your life. While minimalism involves living with less, it actually gives you more than what you are letting go. This lifestyle gives you more space, more time, more peace of mind, and more freedom. Therefore, you shouldn't see this lifestyle as something that will deprive you. Instead, you should see it as a way to appreciate and focus more on the things that truly matter to you.

2. **Minimalism is about intentionality**

   In order to become a minimalist, you should have intentionality, purpose, and clarity. At its very core, minimalism is all about the intention to promote the things that you value the most in your life while eliminating all the things that distract you from those things of value. When you live life as a minimalist, it will force intentionality upon you, thus, creating wonderful improvements in all aspects of your life. Although this is a core principle of minimalism, intentionality isn't the same for everyone. Even if you are able to encourage all the members of your family to follow this path, their intentions will vary greatly from yours. The important thing is to practice deeper introspection so you can discover your true passions and values allowing you to let go of everything else.

3. **Minimalism isn't about restrictions or making your life difficult**

Restricting yourself to the point that you struggle with life or you don't enjoy it anymore is one thing that people are afraid of when it comes to minimalism. Of course, there is no truth to this. Minimalism encourages you to get rid of the things you don't need, the things that are excessive in your life, and even some of the things that make your life more convenient. However, this doesn't mean that you should get rid of everything in a day and focus on restricting your life so you can say that you're living with less. This is not what minimalism is about.

In fact, living life as a minimalist is a lot easier and simpler. For instance, if you don't own a bunch of appliances, you have less to maintain. If you don't have a lot of furniture, you have less to clean. If you don't have a lot of clothes, you don't have a lot to choose from each morning before going to work. After spending some time as a minimalist, you will discover that this simpler life actually brings you more happiness because you won't have to deal with the many complexities that used to come with your life when you had too much.

4. **Minimalism will free you from your passion to possess**

Our modern-day culture has taught us that a good life is all about possessing as many things as possible. Because of this, we believe that the more we have, the happier we will be. But when you achieve success in your career and you can afford to buy everything you think you need, you realize that all of these things don't really add to your happiness. When you embrace minimalism, you will be free of this strong passion to possess, thus, allowing you to focus more on what is important like your relationships, your freedom, your time, and your family. This newfound freedom will show you that you already have everything you need and you can feel grateful for this. In the end, minimalism will give you a more abundant, happier life.

5. Minimalism is for everyone

As long as you want to become a minimalist, you can be one. If the intention is there, you have already won half the battle. There are many things that you could do to start living a minimalist life and you can apply all of these to people of all ages. For instance, one basic strategy of minimalism is decluttering. As a parent, you can do this by getting rid of the things in your home that you don't need. You can encourage your children to do this too by sorting through their things— for instance, their toys—and getting rid of the ones they don't need or want anymore. No matter what steps you have to take to become a minimalist or even a whole household of minimalists, all you have to do is make slight adjustments so that everyone can join in.

When you think about it, minimalism is actually more important for families as it encourages all the members to grow closer together. Through this lifestyle, you can get rid of the things that distract you from each other, thus, allowing you to spend more time with each other and make room for the things that matter most. Even if you all have different personalities, you would share the same core values as a family. So if you can convince your partner, children, and the other members of your family to start adopting this lifestyle, it makes it easier for you to incorporate minimalism into all the aspects of your family life.

Just like intentionality, minimalism looks different for everyone. Even if you explain this concept to the members of your family then ask

14

them to describe it to you, it might surprise you to hear different explanations and descriptions. But the good news is, all the benefits that this lifestyle has to offer apply to everyone who adopts it no matter how different the explanations and interpretations are. This is why it works and this is why it has been around for so long.

A Short History of Minimalism

Minimalism isn't a new concept as it has been mentioned throughout our history. Several religious groups have mentioned the act of denouncing their possessions (which, in essence, is minimalism) to gain wisdom and spiritual focus. The same thing goes for religious leaders who take an oath of poverty allowing them to focus more on their missions and on their people.

Although the concept has been around for some time now, the term 'minimalism' wasn't used until recently. As a matter of fact, the original meaning of the term minimalism had nothing to do with possessions, clutter, or the simple lifestyle we now associate it with. Back in the '50s and '60s, minimalism became popular but still not as a lifestyle. Back then, minimalism was used in the context of music and then in the context of art and design. But it did already have the basic concept of eliminating everything but the design pieces or instruments of focus. When minimalism was popularized in architecture and home design, people started to see the aspects of minimalism that were visually appealing. This was the start of minimalism as a movement toward simplicity.

Then in the year 2010, Nicodemus and Fields Millburn, two public speakers, filmmakers, authors, and podcasters from America started pursuing a minimalist lifestyle. Through this lifestyle, they experienced the benefits of living with less and in December of the same year, they launched their own website where they shared all of their experiences. Then late in 2012, the pair of Americans made the decision to move to Philipsburg, Montana to live in a cabin and focus on writing about the simplistic lifestyle. The pair stayed only four months before moving to Missoula, Montana. Then late in 2017, they moved once again to LA, California to build a studio focused on spreading their message of minimalistic (intentional and simple) living.

Minimalism as a movement has a clear definition—to simplify your life and intentionally live with less. But the way to get there can be customized according to your own needs, preferences, and motivation. Just like Nicodemus, Fields Millburn, and everyone else throughout history who has lived a minimalist life, you can start by setting your intention. From there, things will start to change and you will see why more and more people have chosen to live with less even though modern culture says otherwise.

It's All in the Mind

Minimalism is a lot of things—and it is also a state of mind. Since intentionality is the core idea of minimalism, this means that you can start your journey by setting your intention or setting your mind to it. Then you can start doing the strategies and steps, which we will be discussing later on. Although minimalism is gaining momentum in recent years, it remains to be a negative thing to a lot of people. For such people, they believe that minimalism involves sacrifice and it means surrendering to a simple life instead of taking advantage of all the modern conveniences the world has to offer. But if these people actually tried to learn what minimalism is, they might have a different perception of it.

To live a minimalist life, you should also have a minimalist state of mind. As you live this life, you will feel happier and more content with the things that you have and you won't feel worried about the things that you don't have—or the things that you purposely let go. And the longer you live this type of life, the more you will realize how fulfilling and stress-free it can be.

Right now, try to come up with an image of yourself in your mind living a minimalist life. When asked to do this, a lot of people might picture themselves sitting alone in a small, dark house with nothing but a mattress, a lamp, and a wood-burning stove for cooking. While some people go to such extremes, not all minimalists live like this. As a minimalist myself, I can tell you that there are so many ways you can live this life without having to give up so much that you end up feeling miserable and defeated.

Another way to look at minimalism is valuing yourself, your family, and the other people you love more than your material possessions. This means that when it's time for you to make decisions, you would base these decisions on what you and your family need rather than basing your decisions on your desire to get what you want. However, it doesn't mean that you aren't allowed to buy anything new nor does it mean that when you buy new things, you only opt for the cheapest items. If you need something essential, it's better to purchase a high-quality product instead of buying something cheap that won't last for a long time. Otherwise, you might end up with broken objects in your home that will add to the clutter in your space.

One of the best things about minimalism is that you can decide how much of this lifestyle you want to lead for yourself and your family. You can also start slow and progress gradually at your own pace. For instance, when you make the decision to become a minimalist, you can start by going through all of the appliances in your home. Do this by sorting appliances one room at a time then deciding whether you want to sell or give away the things that you want to get rid of. Then you can move on to your other items like furniture, accessories, clothes, and more. This is an effective way to start becoming a minimalist as it won't pressure you or stress you out.

Keep in mind that minimalism is all about owning fewer things. Think about it: do you really need a closet full of clothes, half of which you don't actually use? Or do you really need all the fancy dishes and silverware that have been sitting in your cupboard waiting for a special occasion that has never come? We are all so used to buying things that

17

we think we need on a whim then storing them for "future use." And we are all so used to storing items because they have some level of sentimental value to us even if we know for a fact that we will never use them again. These habits that you are used to are also the ones that are preventing you from becoming a true minimalist. Difficult as it may seem, if you want minimalism to be your new way of life, it's time for you to break these bad habits. Let go of your previous beliefs and break free from modern mania. It's time to realize that happiness isn't found in material possessions but in ourselves, in the people who matter the most to us, and in things that we cannot buy, own or store in our homes. Minimalism is all in the mind. So if you can convince yourself, adopting this lifestyle will become a lot easier.

CHAPTER 2:

MINIMALISM FOR FAMILIES DONE RIGHT

We all love our families, right?

But this doesn't mean that family life is perfect. These days, families often find themselves fighting with one another, constantly feeling stressed, and they just can't seem to get along with each other at home. In the worst cases, family members feel like there's just no room for everyone at home even though physically, they live in a large house with a lot of space. Also, family members these days find it extremely difficult to prioritize the important things in life. These are some of the most common issues families struggle with and some (if not all) of these issues may sound familiar to you.

The problem with a lot of families these days is that they are focused too much on material things. Parents, children, teens, and even grandparents are obsessed with collecting material possessions to compete with other families and show that they have more. But why do you need to do this? What is the purpose of having a lot of stuff when you don't even feel happiness in the company of your own family? Wouldn't you rather have a whole, happy family than one that's full of shiny things that don't add value to your life?

If having a happier family is something you yearn for, then you should really consider minimalism for families. This is the best solution to living a life of calm where you can easily prioritize your relationships over everything else. Once you can free yourself of the hold material possessions have on you, a life with less stress will come shortly after. Even if you don't do anything drastic to change your life, as long as you do small, significant things each day, you can move in the right direction. And the best part is, all the members of your family can do their part so you can become a family of minimalists.

So, how do you do family minimalism the right way?

It should start with you. Since you're the one reading this book, it means that you're the one who is most interested in becoming a minimalist. While you have this drive to lead a simpler life, you should learn everything that you can about it. Once you understand what true minimalism entails and you've acquired the minimalist mindset, then you can start influencing the other members of your family. Changing your own mindset is already an achievement in itself. And this can be your first step towards creating a happier, healthy minimalist family.

The Downside of Family Life

Having a family is a wonderful thing. But there are times when living with your family can feel very draining, especially if you are all looking for or expecting something more from each other. Sad as it may be, a lot of people feel this way about their family and some of the main causes of this dire situation are social media, technology, too many things to do, too little time for each other, and an abundance of clutter. All of these result in a number of problems within the family which, in turn, can start destroying your relationships.

Over time, parents treat each other with disdain, children stop listening to their parents and start feeling resentful towards them, one partner loses respect for their spouse and even may start looking for affection from other people, and so on. All of these negative effects will start snowballing until you wake up one day to a broken family. And the worst part is, you can't even find peace in your own home because there is too much clutter there. While nobody wants this to happen to their own family, knowing the most common issues families face is important as it makes you more aware of where your family stands right now and what can potentially bring your family down. Knowing these issues enables you to avoid them more effectively, especially as you are trying to adopt a minimalist life.

1. **Money is always a huge issue because "there is never enough"**

Money is always a huge issue when it comes to relationships. It can ruin friendships, it can push people to betray those who trust them, it can cause those desperate for it to take another person's life, and more. If you let it, money can also destroy your family. Whether you live on the poverty line, in the middle class or upper class, money will always be an issue—because when it comes to money, there never seems to be enough.

Try to think about the last time you experienced a financial problem. When you were young and single, this would have already been devastating. Now that you have a family, money problems become even more problematic. When you have grown used to a life of comfort and luxury, anything that threatens your financial situation will definitely cause you a lot of stress. This is normal. But you should never take this out on your spouse, your children, or any other members of your family. Instead, you should learn how to deal with these financial challenges together so they don't break your family apart.

Or you can also minimize the threat of financial issues by adopting a minimalist lifestyle. Instead of spending your money on things that you don't really need, save it. As a minimalist, you won't feel the obsession to accumulate material possessions. And if the rest of your family feels the same way, you'll realize that the money you (and your spouse) are earning is actually more than enough to support your whole family. It's all about learning how to spend your money wisely so it doesn't have to be a downside in your family.

2.   Spouses start neglecting each other

This is one issue that is commonly caused by all the distractions around us. Whether it be your work, the chores you have to do at home, your responsibilities as a parent, and more, all of these things make you so busy that you end up neglecting the person you're supposed to be building your family with—your spouse. And when your spouse feels like you don't care about them anymore, you don't have time for them or you are focusing on other things instead of them, this can lead to a lot of bad things like vices, indifference, and even infidelity.

The good news is, minimalism can help you with this issue too. When you adopt a minimalist lifestyle, you will learn how to declutter your life. You won't keep buying things just to keep occupied, you will stop trying to do everything just to please everyone, and you will start focusing on your relationships more. When you're not distracted or busy with other things, you can go back to focusing on your children and your spouse. Spend time with them, care for them, and show them that you are present with them and for them all the time. Never neglect your spouse. That is, unless you want them to start neglecting you too.

3.   Parents aren't being responsible enough

Aside from spousal neglect, there are also times when parents start forgetting their responsibilities to their children. Again, this can happen when you are too busy with other things or you are too focused on earning money to accumulate a lot of wealth. As your children grow, they need you to be there. As a parent, it's your responsibility to make sure that your children get what they need all the time—and this includes your time, attention, presence, and love.

Don't allow yourself to be overwhelmed by trying to do too many things to the point that your children are left to fend for themselves. When this happens, your children might encounter problems that place them in dangerous situations. And if you're not there to support them or help them out, you might lose your children in more ways than one. Reduce the clutter in your life to give you more time to spend nurturing and communicating with your children. This is one of the most significant things you can do as part of your minimalist lifestyle to make your family stronger.

4. **No gratitude, appreciation, and communication between family members**

    These three things are crucial to family life. Without gratitude, appreciation, and communication, there is a very high likelihood that the feelings that will exist between you and the rest of your family members will only be negative. Try to think about the last time you did something nice for your spouse or for one of your children. How did they react? If they thanked you and gave you a hug because of what you did, that would have made you feel wonderful. But what if they didn't even notice your nice gesture because they were too distracted or busy? Chances are, you would have felt bad about it and you might have even felt resentment towards them.

    Fortunately, minimalism promotes gratitude, appreciation, and communication within families. If you live with less, you learn how to appreciate each other more and feel more grateful for the things you do for each other no matter how small. In the same way, when you don't have televisions with intriguing shows, electronic devices with fun games, and social media platforms with interesting content, there is a higher likelihood that you would start communicating with the people in your home. The less you have, the more you can focus on the people around you. And this is what will make your connections deeper and stronger.

You may have noticed a pattern when it comes to the downsides of

23

family life. Whether it be money, neglect, distractions, or whatever, a lot of these problems stem from having too much while still feeling like you don't have enough. This is why minimalism is so great for families. Through this lifestyle, you can get rid of toxic feelings, thus, making your family happier and your home more stress-free.

Turning Your Family's Situation Around

If you are experiencing any of the issues in the last section, it's time to turn things around for the better. Minimalism can be the solution to your family's problems because it allows you to let go of material possessions and other things that don't contribute to your family's life. Through minimalism, you will learn how to live a life filled with respect, gratitude, and appreciation towards each other.

Did you know that clutter can come in different forms? Clutter doesn't just refer to the things in your home that take up space. It can also be your endless to-do lists, your busy calendar, your fear of losing the things that make your life comfortable, the constant discontent you feel in your life, the mindless browsing that takes up your time, and so much more. Clutter takes the form of anything that distracts you and your family from a life of intention and meaning. Therefore, to turn your family's situation around and towards minimalism, follow these steps:

1. **Define what is really important in your life**

    This is the most important step you should take towards a minimalist life. Defining the things that you value in your life helps you determine what to keep and what you can let go of. To do this, spend time reflecting by yourself and have conversations with your spouse and the rest of your family about it. Once you define what truly matters, the other steps become easier and more manageable.

2. **Break your shopping habit**

    Look around your home right now and try to think about the

things that you need and the things that you don't. Chances are, most of the things you see in your home are just there as clutter. In most homes in this modern day and age, about 80% of the material things aren't actually used. From kitchen appliances to furniture, decorations, and more, all of these things exist in your home because you couldn't stop yourself from buying them. If you want to become a minimalist, it's time to break your habit of shopping.

Unless you or one of your family members really needs something, don't buy it. In fact, you should never buy things right away even if you think you need them. Give yourself time to really reflect on the item before you purchase it. For instance, if one of your chairs at home breaks, don't rush to the furniture store right away. Instead, take an inventory of the other chairs in your home. Do you really need to buy another chair or can you and your family make do with one less chair?

When something breaks or gets worn out at home, the usual solution most people have is to buy a new item. But this isn't always the best or most practical solution, especially if you want to become a minimalist. Stop buying things all the time if you want to reduce the clutter in your home. This is another important step to take towards minimalism and it's one that will help you long-term.

3. **Don't focus on organizing things right away**

At this stage, organizing won't be very helpful, especially if you haven't gotten rid of anything you own yet. If you try to organize your stuff now, you'll just be moving and sorting things from one place to another. Don't worry, there will be time to organize. But this will come after you have decluttered your life a bit and rid yourself of unnecessary things. In fact, when you have more space at home because of the things you have sold or given away, it will become a lot easier to organize. So be patient. There is still more to do.

4. **Avoid the things that waste your time**

Becoming a minimalist is a process, not something you can accomplish overnight. Therefore, you should really set a schedule for yourself to incorporate minimalist tips and strategies into your routine each day. During the first few weeks, you may want to focus on getting rid of the things you don't need and this includes activities that tend to distract you and take up too much of your time such as:

o   Watching television
o   Playing games on your phone or tablet
o   Too many clothes to choose from, wash, fold, and store

These are just some examples of time wasters that you should consider getting rid of. Remember that minimalism is also about freeing up your schedule so you have free time to spend with your family. Therefore, if there are activities or things in your home that take you away from this, you may want to consider getting rid of them.

5. **Start rekindling your relationships**

This doesn't just apply to your relationship with your spouse. If you are part of a family, you should value each member equally—from your partner to your youngest child. If the realization that your family life isn't what you wanted or expected it to be and you want to make things better through minimalism, then you should make a conscious effort to start rekindling your relationships. After spending time decluttering and self-reflecting, spend some quality time with your family and really be there for them. This will go a long way into improving your family life while also making it easier for your family to see how minimalism can make things better at home.

In a world where accumulating material possessions is easy and convenient, being able to control the amount of clutter in your home is a challenge. But as long as you have a strong purpose, intentionality, and patience, you will eventually find your true path to a minimalist life for yourself and your family.

Transforming Your Family's Life With Minimalism

Minimalism isn't a one-time solution to your family's problems. It's a movement, a lifestyle, and a series of tips and strategies that you can apply to your life to make it simpler and less stressful. Once you set your mind to becoming a minimalist, you can start embracing this lifestyle and taking the necessary steps to achieve it. Right now, take some time to relax, reflect, and get comfortable with the idea of living with less. If this thought makes you uncomfortable or stressed, you might struggle to apply the tips that you have learned and will learn in the next chapters. If you're not yet feeling this lifestyle and you don't think that you can make a big change, that's okay. It's better to start small and stay consistent than try to do something big then end up regretting things.

For instance, you can start with one area of your home. If you're an avid reader, start by going through your book collection and picking out the ones that you haven't read in a long time and don't plan to read anymore. Place all of these books in a box and donate them. Simple as this exercise is, it's already a step towards minimalism. Since customization is one feature of minimalism, you can start with activities you feel comfortable with then work from there. When you're ready, you can start doing these tips on your own or with the other members of your family:

1. **Think of your why**

    In the previous section, the first tip I shared was to define the things that matter to you. The next thing you must do is think about *why* you want to become a minimalist. Now it comes time for self-reflection and introspection. As you're reading this book, you must already have a reason for wanting to live a simpler life. Now, you should write it down as a future reminder each time you encounter a bump in the road.

You can also share this purpose of yours with your family. After all, one of your goals is to encourage your whole family to become minimalists, right? When you share your own reason for wanting this big change, you can show them why your family needs minimalism to be and feel better. Then you can ask the other members of your family for possible reasons why they would get on board with you. As you have this sharing session, write down all the reasons and ideas that come out. When you see all of your reasons, these will, hopefully, convince you to work hand-in-hand to become a family of minimalists together.

2. Look for—and discard—any duplicate items you own

This is a great step to take that will surely free up space in your home. Without even knowing it, you and your family might have been buying the same things and storing them along with the rest of the clutter. For this activity, you can do it as a family or you can do it alone with consent from your spouse and children. Take a box or a bag then move from one room to another collecting any duplicates that you find.

For instance, if you go through your linen closet and see that you have two of the same blanket, place one of them in the box. Or if you go through your clothes and see that you have duplicate sweaters or shirts (not exactly alike but similar to each other), place those in your box too. If you have a large house and a lot of stuff, you can do this one room or area at a time. You also have the option to go through your whole house in one go but this might prove to be an exhausting task. Either way, it's entirely up to you. Just make sure that if you aren't able to finish in a day, you continue with the task until you've gone through all the rooms in your house and found all duplicate items. Then you can decide whether to sell these things or give them away.

3. **Declare one area or room in your home that should be completely free of clutter**

    If you have a big house, you can set up one of the rooms to be the clutter-free zone. As a family, go through the room and empty it leaving only the bare essentials. After this, make sure that all the members of your family know that this room should always be free of clutter. Eventually, you can make all the rooms in your home clutter-free but the mere fact that you already have such a space in your home will make a huge difference.

    If you don't have room to spare, your clutter-free zone can be something as small as one of the drawers in your bedroom, your nightstand, the kitchen table, a coffee table, and so on. Assign a surface to be completely clutter-free until you all get used to it. This makes it easier for you to understand what a clutter-free zone is, thus, allowing you to treat other spaces and surfaces in your home the same way.

4. **Challenge yourself by "dressing with less"**

    This is one exercise you can do to practice living with fewer clothes. Instead of throwing away or donating all of your clothes right away, choose one outfit per day for one whole month. Then rotate between these outfits for three months. Keep all of the items of clothing you have chosen in one closet and whenever you go out, only choose from that selection. While a lot of people might see this as restricting, you may discover that it's actually easier to dress yourself each morning because you don't have too many clothes to choose from. After three months, you can look at your closet with a new perspective and start sorting through it with more willingness to let things go.

5. **Start a habit of saving**

    As a minimalist, you should start an emergency fund for unexpected occurrences. In fact, even those who aren't planning to adopt minimalism should do this. While budgeting your income each month, make sure that part of it goes into your emergency fund. That way, if anything happens and you need money to get you out of a tough situation, you have a place to get that money from. Just make sure that you only use that money for emergencies that matter—not for impulse buying or shopping sprees when your favorite shops have a sale.

While you can do all of these minimalist tips with your whole family, don't force them into it. You can introduce the concept to them but if they're not ready to live a simpler life, you can start by showing them what it means and how it improves your life. There's no point in coercing your family into minimalism as this will make it a negative experience for them. Just explain your 'why' to them and assure them that if they want to take small steps with you, they can do so with full support and encouragement from you.

CHAPTER 3:

TRANSFORMING YOUR HOME

Your home is where you and your family spend most of your time together. And if your home is a place of clutter and negative feelings, minimalism can help transform this into a place filled with love, contentment, appreciation, and happiness. This is why minimalists devote so much of their ideology for creating the right environment at home. Instead of seeing this as just a place where you keep your things or take shelter from the outside world, it's time to see your home as a living being. One that's forever changing, thus, needs exactly what the people inside need—good maintenance, decluttering, and space.

Can you remember the first day you moved into your home? Back then, it was filled only with the essentials and it felt like a dream. The place where you will be raising your children and building your family. As time goes by, you may acquire a lot of possessions, memories (both good and bad), and people as your family grew one child at a time. All of these have added to the clutter in your home and now, it looks and feels radically different from the home you had first moved into. All of these changes are normal and they don't always have to be a bad thing. That is unless the clutter starts affecting your relationships and turning your home into something unappealing. There are some common reasons why this happens:

- **The memories of your family have turned into visual chaos**

31

Whenever you share milestones, trips, and new experiences with your family, you want to immortalize these through photos. Then you have these photos printed, framed, and scattered all around your home for everyone to see. While this is a wonderful way to keep your memories alive, over time, all of those memories will add to the clutter and visual chaos of your home. When this happens, the space becomes too overwhelming and overstimulating, thus, adding to the stress that you feel.

- **You have accumulated too many material things**

  This is one thing most if not all families are guilty of. You buy new appliances, equipment, furniture, and other material possessions for each member of your family. Naturally, all of these things will end up in your home whether inside storage spaces or on any available surface. As you buy more and more things, your home becomes more cluttered. Then you will reach a point where you don't think you can buy anything else because you don't know where to put it!

- **Distractions can be found everywhere**

  Televisions, cellphones, electronic gadgets, and books make up most of the things you have purchased for each of the members of your family. While you would have bought all of these items to please your spouse or your children, these things are actually tearing your family apart. Sadly, when a family spends more time with their things than with each other, they cannot give each other the love and appreciation they deserve.

The good news is, no matter how dire or hopeless your home situation may seem right now, there is always room for transformation. As long as you want things to change and you're willing to do something about it, you can change your home into a place of love instead of an empty shell.

When a House Isn't a Home

You shouldn't allow your home to become a facade for others to see and believe that a happy family resides inside. Instead of buying so many things to make your home seem abundant, try focusing on the people you share your home with. How many times have you thrown out and replaced a piece of equipment or furniture just because it's out of shape? Or how often do you shop for clothes, toys, and other items just because they are worn out? For a lot of people, their default solution is to buy new things. And when your house is overrun with these things, it stops becoming a home. Here are some factors that can cause you stress at home even if you live with your entire family:

1. **Too much clutter**

   The more clutter you have in your home, the more stressed you will feel. This is especially true when you have spent a long, hard day at work and you come home to a huge mess. Cluttered homes aren't ideal for raising a family. When you constantly have to deal with cluttered spaces, this causes you to feel stressed which, in turn, may cause you to start taking out your frustrations on one another. Fortunately, this isn't something you have to worry about once you start living a minimalist life.

2. **More furniture than you need**

   When any of the rooms in your home contain too many pieces of furniture, this will make you feel stressed and crowded. Your home will feel overstuffed and you can hardly move. And when you're bumping into things because there's no space to move around, this can cause conflicts and arguments. This is why decluttering should also include furniture once you start practicing minimalism.

3. **Messy clothes in an overflowing closet**

   When you have too many clothes, it's always a challenge to keep all of them organized inside your closet. It's a challenge to decide what to wear, it's frustrating when children (or even your spouse) throw their dirty clothes on the floor for you to pick up, it's exhausting to wash so many clothes, it's time-consuming to fold and iron everything you have washed, and when you see that closets are still messy and overflowing with clothes, this can definitely set you off. While clothes are a necessity, having too many in your home will surely add to the clutter and the stress that goes with it.

4. **Indifference between the members of the family**

Finally, and most importantly, a house will never feel like a home if you don't have good relationships with the people in it. When you focus too much on material things, you end up neglecting the people you live with and this is very sad. Your home should be the one place where you all feel happy, safe, and connected with your family. Think about it: how would you feel if you came home after a long, stressful day and nobody even greets you when you come in? Then as you walk through your home, you spot the members of your family lost in their own worlds while your dinner is waiting for you on the dining table. A single table setting just for you because they have all eaten already.

Wouldn't that kind of situation make you feel even more stressed? Imagine how you would feel if the same thing happens every day. This is another thing you must transform on your path towards minimalism. Connecting with your family is important as it will strengthen your family bonds so you can confidently say that you live in a happy home with your loving family.

Less Is More

If you want to transform your house into a minimalist home, you must learn how to simplify it. A minimalist home is basic, efficient, and functional. It is more than shelter and it will thrive when the people inside it (meaning you and your family) thrive too. You need to care for your home and give it constant attention. If there is anything you should place value apart from your family, it is your home.

You may have heard how scientific studies have suggested that messy people tend to be smarter. However, scientific studies have also shown that people who live in places with a lot of clutter, especially women, tend to have high levels of cortisol—the stress hormone. If you have a lot of clutter in your home, you would have to include the task of keeping your home clean in your daily routine. But if you have a busy schedule, how will you manage this time-consuming task? If you're tired of dealing with the issue of clutter, just remember the mantra of minimalism: less is more.

One part of becoming a minimalist is to pare things down to the essentials. Getting rid of superfluous things will do wonders for your home and your stress levels. Plus, if you have ever seen minimalist homes, you will note how sleek and sophisticated they are. And this is because minimalists don't own a lot of things. Instead, their homes have a lot of space to breathe, think, relax, and connect with their families.

But achieving a minimalist home isn't a simple task. It's not just about throwing everything you own out as this might make you feel stressed too. Remember that minimalism is about intentionality. When you simply get rid of everything, you might regret it in the future. You need to think about the things to get rid of and the things to keep. That way, you don't end up with a home that is devoid of personality, life, and fun. Getting rid of things should make you feel good about the improvements you are making to your life. Also, the "less is more" lifestyle offers the following benefits:

- **It makes your home more appealing to live in**

   Minimalist homes are clean, efficient, and spacious. But this doesn't mean that minimalist homes are large. Because we only keep what we need—not even the things that add convenience to our lives—all of these things would have their own places. Nothing in excess means that nothing overflows, nothing is out of place, and there is no clutter to make you feel frustrated.

- **Cleaning is a lot easier**

  Naturally, when there is no clutter, cleaning becomes much easier. When your home only contains the essentials, all you have to worry about is keeping the floors clean, keeping surfaces free of dust, and organizing your own personal belongings. Then you can teach your children to organize their things too. If they don't own a lot of material things, keeping everything organized is an easy task even for young children.

- **It's less stressful**

  Keep in mind that clutter can take many forms. In your home, clutter makes you feel visually distracted, thus, you won't be able to give your full attention to your family. But if you adopt minimalism and reduce the clutter in your home, the less visual stress you will have. This, in turn, makes you feel calmer, less stressed, and more willing to strike up conversations with the members of your family.

Your minimalist lifestyle doesn't have to happen overnight. Start with the mindset, create a plan, then take small steps each day to declutter your home to make it suitable for the lifestyle you're trying to have.

The Minimalist Home and How To Achieve It

Just because our modern-day lifestyles are the exact opposite of minimalism, this doesn't mean that you have no choice but to conform. Despite the abundance of distractions around us, you can still modify your home to make it a space where you and your family can really communicate and be yourselves no matter how chaotic or stressful the outside world becomes. Allowing yourself to be overwhelmed with the mental, physical, and digital clutter of the modern world will chip away at your sanity until there's nothing left but negativity. For this, minimalism can be the antidote to make you feel better and more satisfied with your life. Since the main environment of your family is your home, this is where you should start making changes. Here are some ways to achieve the minimalist home of your dreams:

1. **Minimal furniture**

   In your minimalist home, each of the rooms should only contain a few pieces of furniture. For instance, in your living room, you may only have a couch, one or two more chairs, a center table, a simple entertainment center with a television, and a simple light fixture. These are basic pieces of furniture that allow you to spend time as a family in the room together without having extravagant or unnecessary things.

2. **Clutter-free surfaces**

   All the surfaces of your minimalist home should be free of clutter. Surfaces like tables, shelves, and more can contain simple decorations but never things that don't belong on them like books, bags, documents, and even random knick-knacks that don't add to the aesthetic of the room.

3. **Simple decorations**

   Minimalist homes can have decorations too to make things more interesting. For instance, in your living room, the center table can have a small but interesting centerpiece or even a vase with fresh flowers that you replace every day. You can also scatter a few photo frames around your house that contain the best memories you shared as a family. When it comes to decorating your minimalist home, here are a few tips for you:

   o Hang simple pieces of art that mainly have solid, subdued colors that match the rest of the room's color scheme.

   o Simple window treatments such as wooden blinds or curtains with solid colors.

   o Furniture, carpets, and other accessories that have plain patterns and solid colors that complement each other.

   o Subtle and subdued colors throughout the house. While

you can have a piece of furniture or a decorative item that adds a splash of color to the room, it should mostly have colors that are easy on the eyes.

After you have simplified each of the rooms in your home, you don't have to stop there. Just keep editing, adding, and eliminating as needed until you feel content and comfortable no matter which room you spend time in.

4. Cohesiveness from one room to another

Once you have worked on the furniture, surfaces, and decorations of your home, try to see if everything flows together cohesively from one room to another. This means that no matter what room you go into, you will always feel like you are in your home. Conversely, if you enter one of the rooms and it feels like everything is different, this means that it lacks cohesiveness. Again, you can add things, remove things, rearrange things, and more until you achieve cohesiveness throughout your home.

5. Focus on quality instead of quantity

Rather than having a lot of low-quality items in your home, choose things that you really need and the ones you always use. For instance, you can choose a nice, sturdy table over a 5-piece set of press-board furniture that won't last for a long time. Apply this tip to furniture, appliances, equipment, and even gadgets in your home. Choosing quality over quantity all the time ensures that you will own things for years to come without having to replace them because they get broken, damaged, or worn-out too easily.

6. Work on decluttering one room at a time

I have mentioned decluttering a couple of times already and I will keep mentioning this throughout the book because this is one of the most significant things that you should do to become a minimalist. When decluttering your home, do this one room at a time. It's virtually impossible to declutter your whole house in a day, especially if you have never practiced minimalism in the past. Start with your own room or with the room that contains the most clutter. Create a schedule if you have to. Just make sure that when you start decluttering one room, you continue until you have covered all the other rooms in the house. Otherwise, you might just be moving things from one room to another without actually getting rid of anything!

7. Think about the essential items you need in each room

This is another important step to make your home simpler. As you start decluttering and organizing the rooms in your home, think about how you can optimize functionality. For instance, as you declutter in your kitchen, leave everything but the essentials. Does your kitchen need a television? No. Does your kitchen need a stove? Yes. Does your kitchen need an extra table? If you don't have enough space for preparing ingredients while cooking, yes. But if you have enough space to prepare, cook, and store all the basic kitchen items, no, you don't need an extra table. It's all about determining what you really need in the specific rooms in your home to make them as basic yet functional as possible.

8. Be very strict when it comes to bringing in new things

Never buy things on impulse or just because they are on sale. After decluttering your home, give yourself time to get used to having more space and fewer things. Just because your home has become more spacious, this doesn't mean that you should go out and replace everything you got rid of. This is where you should start practicing the minimalist mindset. In cases where you feel tempted to buy something new, think carefully if you really need it. Think about which room to put it in, think about where you will put it, and think about whether or not you will really use it. Often, after long consideration, you will end up not buying the items that initially caught your eye.

9. **Clean your home**

Part of maintaining your home is ensuring that it is always clean. Make sure that your floors are completely clean and clutter-free. Don't stack anything on the floor, don't store anything on the floor, and always make sure that you sweep and mop regularly. The same thing goes for the clear surfaces in your home. It's not enough to have clear surfaces, you should clean them too. That way, you don't have to deal with dusty surfaces that can make you or the rest of your family sick. Remember that cleaning actually becomes an easier task in a minimalist home. This means that you don't need to spend a lot of time and effort in cleaning, especially if you do it regularly.

10. **Store things you don't use regularly**

If you don't have the heart or the time to get rid of things right away, you can store them first. A minimalist home shouldn't have clutter; thus, you can choose to set one room in your house where you place all unessential things to be sorted at a later date. Just make sure that you don't store those items in one room permanently. After you have gone through all the rooms in your home, the next thing to do is to declutter and organize your storage room. That way, you can still get rid of all the things you don't need while giving yourself time to make things easier.

All of these tips are very simple, but doing them will help you create a minimalist home. Since minimalism is all about the bare essentials, the whole process will take time, effort, and a lot of reflection. As you are intentionally getting rid of things you don't need and keeping things that add value to your life, you will also learn how to appreciate these things more. Don't rush through this process. Slow down and savor each moment as you remind yourself that you are doing these things to improve your family's life. After transforming your home, you can start working on your relationships with each member of your family.

CHAPTER 4:

STRENGTHENING FAMILY BONDS THROUGH MINIMALISM

Relationships are complicated things, even the relationships that exist between family members. To have the best possible relationship with your spouse, your children, or any other family members, you have to play a constant game of trial and error to find out what doesn't work and what does. Over time, relationships grow stronger, and when you make mistakes, you learn valuable lessons. One important part of your journey towards minimalism is to make your family bonds stronger. Through minimalism, you can learn how to become a better spouse, a better parent, or even a better child.

If you were single and you lived in a small home, it would be easier to transition to a minimalist life. However, when you are part of a family, trying to get rid of everything in your home is neither simple nor practical. Before we move on, you should remember that minimalism doesn't mean that you have to force yourself and your family to live with a very small amount of stuff. This line of thinking will give you the wrong idea, and it might cause you a lot of stress as you try to force your spouse or your children to get rid of the things that they need. We have already defined minimalism and gone through some steps to start living a more minimalist life. Now, it's time to incorporate these things into your role as a spouse, parent, or child to help the rest of your family understand how minimalism will make things better.

To become a true minimalist, you have to find your "sweet spot." Remember that minimalism comes with guidelines and suggested strategies, not with strict rules that everyone has to follow to the tee. Minimalism is entirely customizable, thus, allowing you to keep just the right number of items that you need. To live a simpler life, you don't have to get rid of everything you own for the sake of showing the world that you can still continue living despite having nothing. For minimalism to work in your family, it must be practical. It shouldn't be too extreme that you make your life unpleasant or difficult for everyone else. Consider these examples of situations where minimalism is taken to the extreme, thus, making it a negative thing for the whole family:

- Minimizing the amount of food in your home to ensure that there is no food waste. However, you have to go shopping each day just so your family will have something to eat.
- You only choose one color to paint the whole house and all of the rooms so you can save on paint. While this might seem like a good idea, it might feel stressful for you and the rest of your family to only see a single color throughout the house no matter what room you're in. Minimalism doesn't mean that you have to make your room look like a prison.
- You get rid of all 'excess' clothes to the point that you have to do laundry every single night so that you all have clean clothes to wear the next day.
- You throw out all of your books, board games, and other items that you enjoy together as a family so that you have more time to bond and have conversations with each other.

Such situations would definitely cause frustration and tension in your family—and this will inevitably happen when you go beyond what's necessary and what's right for your family. Minimalism should be a pleasant, positive, and enriching process. It should be something that brings your family closer. Therefore, in this chapter, we will go through the family aspect of minimalism and how you can make this lifestyle work to everyone's benefit.

All About Family Relationships

The most important part of a healthy family is the relationships that exist between each of the members. The time that you spend with your family is one of the most valuable gifts you can ever give to them. But this can be extremely difficult, especially if you have gotten used to the distractions in your home. Because of these distractions, you may have grown comfortable living in solitude, although the rest of your family shares the same home with you. In fact, for some families, they first have to go through horrible events like accidents or divorce before they realize how important their relationships are.

As you get rid of the clutter in your life through minimalism, you should also learn how to replace this clutter with more important things. Since one of your main goals is to make your family life better, one thing you can replace your clutter with is your relationships. Learn how to prioritize and nurture your relationships to make them stronger. When this improvement in relationships starts with you, the rest of your family members will also feel encouraged to follow suit. Soon, you will realize that your family has grown closer, and you share more profound relationships with each other. But before you can do this, you should recognize the signs that your family is undergoing problems. To work on making your relationships better, you must deal with existing issues first. Some of the most common issues that cause rifts in your relationships are:

1. **When one member has a strong need for dominance and power**

   Usually, this is felt by one of the parents, although children may feel this too (especially teenagers). All families have dominant members and less dominant members. But if one of the dominant members wants everyone else to follow everything they say, that will cause some tension. For instance, if one of the parents gets involved in a conflict with another family member, it might make them upset. When this happens, the parent might exert his control and power by ordering everyone else to cut-off communications with that family member. Naturally, if the family member involved is close to the rest of the family, they might not want to cut-off communication. This will cause a lot of stress, which, if left unresolved, will also lead to negative feelings.

If you have one such member in your family, you should have a conversation with them. Things need to change for life to become better within your family. If you are the person who is overly dominant in the family, then you should take steps to change how you interact with your family. This will take time and a lot of effort, but it will go a long way into making your family happier and more positive.

2. When one family member makes others feel exhausted

There are certain people who can make others feel depleted or exhausted, even without trying too hard. For instance, if your spouse finds parenting too difficult and they become extremely pessimistic. Even the smallest things set them off, and they end up taking out their frustrations on you or worse, on your children. This is another issue that you have to deal with first before starting your minimalist journey.

Imagine how difficult it would be to convince your spouse to get rid of things you don't need when they are already very pessimistic? In such a case, there is a very high likelihood that there will be a lot of arguments and resistance, especially from your spouse or any other family member who is similarly exhausting. Therefore, you may want to help this family member first before you make any big changes in your life.

3. Lack of loyalty

This is one of the most devastating issues you can encounter, especially if it happens between spouses. Sometimes, when family issues get too overwhelming, one spouse tries to find comfort in another person instead of dealing with the issues at home. Lack of loyalty may also manifest when a teenager chooses their friends or boy/girlfriend over their family.

Generally, though, a lack of loyalty happens because there is also a lack of communication between family members. Be brave enough to reach out, especially when you feel like there is an issue troubling one of the members of your family. Loyalty doesn't just happen—you should love and nurture each other so that you will all feel loyalty and trust towards each other no matter what challenges come your way.

4. **Financial issues**

Financial issues are one of the most common issues families deal with today. Parents, spouses, children, and other members of the family can experience difficulties when it comes to money. When there isn't enough money, this leads to a lot of frustration. But even if there is a lot of money, the problems don't stop. Fortunately, this is one problem that you can deal with through minimalism. When you take your focus off material things (including money), it won't be that much of a problem anymore. Also, when you learn how to live within your means through minimalism, you won't feel like you don't have enough money to sustain your family.

5. **Abusive family members**

Sadly, so many people have been abused physically, emotionally, verbally, or psychologically by the members of their family. The effects of abuse don't go away easily and some even carry the repercussions of these experiences until they grow up. No matter what form it comes in, abuse must stop. If needed, ask for professional help to deal with this issue. Otherwise, you won't be able to achieve your goal of having a happy, loving family.

6. **Other issues**

   Apart from these common issues, there are others that are considered 'minor' but that you may also want to deal with before or during your journey towards minimalism. Some of these include:

   o   Significant changes or events like a new baby, separation, relatives living with the family, and more
   o   A difference in beliefs, values or opinions
   o   Issues related to the sexuality of any of the family members
   o   Problems with alcohol, gambling, or drug use
   o   The onset of medical conditions or mental health issues
   o   Natural disasters
   o   Lack of respect between the members of the family

Any of these issues (and other issues that aren't mentioned here) can cause a lot of stress on the family and strain on the relationships that exist between family members. You may have the best intentions as you try to implement changes for minimalism in your home and family. Still, unless you deal with the issues first, you might find it extremely challenging to transition into minimalism successfully.

It's Time to Get Real

When it comes to using minimalism to improve your family life, another important thing you can do is learn how to "get real" with your family. The more authentic you are, the more you can share with them. It's time to get rid of the image of false perfection that you have kept for the longest time. When you are part of a family, staying true to your situation is key to maintaining a healthy household. On the other hand, when you try to keep things from the other members of your family, this will only cause strain on your relationships, especially when the truth eventually comes out.

Because of the fast pace of the world we live in, personal connection is slowly becoming a thing of the past. Even when you share the same dinner table with your family, you might not be present with them as you browse through various social media platforms while you consume your meal. And the sad part is, everyone else is doing the same thing. But the beauty of minimalism is that you will learn how to focus on the people around you instead of on the things that surround you. Part of this process is learning how to get real with your family and here are some ways to do this:

- **Start off fresh**

  It's virtually impossible to start a new process of improvement when you keep focusing on the past. After dealing with the issues that have plagued your family, you can start your minimalist journey off fresh. Doing this makes the process more comfortable as it doesn't come with unnecessary baggage or negative feelings that can become more significant problems along the way.

  Minimalism is all about getting rid of things you don't need, and this includes the problems you had in the past. When you start off fresh, you will also have a new perspective, thus, making you more open to suggestions like the ones in this book or any other ideas that may come from the other members of your family.

- **Practice being real**

  As a minimalist, you should place more value on authenticity over your image of what other people think of you. You have to work on this by practicing it every chance that you get. When faced with situations, think about how you—the real you—should respond to it. Think about how you want to respond to the situation, not how you think you should respond to it because of what other people expect of you.

  This step may take some getting used to, but with more practice, the more this becomes your natural response. Soon, you will be the most authentic member of your family, and, hopefully, the other members of your family will feel inspired to act the same way.

- **Have the courage to ask difficult questions**

  To become a real minimalist, you should be able to ask yourself even the most difficult questions. You should also have the courage to ask your family these questions so that you can eventually learn how to let go of the emotions tied to your material possessions and only focus on functionality. As you practice the other strategies to become a minimalist, the most basic questions to ask yourself (and your family) are:

  o Is this essential?
  o Is this the only thing of its type that you have?
  o Does this item bring you love, joy, or happiness?

  If you answer 'yes' to all of these questions, then you won't have to get rid of the item in question. If not, it's time to let the item go. This is another step to take for you to bring out your most authentic self.

- **Learn how to let things go**

  Here's another important step that you should master in order to become a true minimalist. When decluttering, you should learn how to let go of your material possessions. When solving problems with your family, you should learn how to let go of ill feelings. The list goes on. The only thing that you should never let go of is the relationships you have with the people in your family.

- **Live in the moment**

  This is an essential part of being real. This entails experiencing each moment as it unfolds with acceptance and understanding. For instance, if you're in the process of decluttering your child's room, be there as this happens. That way, you can help your child get rid of the things they don't need by asking difficult questions.

The same thing goes for when you're sharing moments with your family. For instance, as you sit together for dinner, have conversations with them. Listen to what they have to say so you can react and respond accordingly. Living in the moment with the people you love the most is another way to bring you closer to them and nurture deeper connections.

- **Focus on family connections**

    Remember that minimalism will help you focus more on your family instead of the things that you own. Enjoy this benefit as it is the one that will bring true joy to your life. Your connections are the building blocks of your family. And when you get real with them, you can focus more on the connections that exist between you.

The Best Minimalist Practices to Strengthen Family Relationships

We have already gone through some practical and effective minimalist strategies in the previous chapters. Now, let's go through three essential minimalist practices that will help you ensure that you are always giving your best when it comes to strengthening the relationships you have with your family. Whether you're the spouse, mother, father, or child in the family, these minimalist practices will help you become the best family member you can possibly be. Just practice these regularly to help yourself improve as the days go by:

- **Practice 1: Be yourself no matter what situation you are faced with**

    We have already discussed the importance of being real, especially with your family. The moment you step through the door of your home, leave your mask, your pretensions, and your social image at the door. There is no need for you to try to impress your family because they know who you are and they value you for it. Your family should accept everything about you and you should do the same for them. Start practicing being yourself no matter what situation you are faced with at home.

When it comes to making decisions, solving problems, dealing with conversations, and even decluttering, make sure that you do all of these as yourself and nobody else. If you need support, turn to your family. If you need help, ask them for it. And always make sure that when they need to be themselves while facing challenges, you will also be there to support and help them as needed. It's all about being authentic and only keeping the things that are valuable in your life. If you want your family to become stronger and you want to draw in the "right people" to your life, just be yourself. You are enough and you should believe this.

In terms of becoming a minimalist, being yourself means taking the high ground when faced with materialism. As you declutter, you should be honest with yourself and only keep the things you really need and those that bring value to your life. Get rid of the notion that you should impress other people by owning more material possessions than others. If you sincerely want to practice minimalism, stick with the basics, then place more effort into cultivating your relationships with your family and the other people you have in your life.

- **Practice 2: Let go of your emotional clutter**

I have already mentioned how clutter can take many forms. The most common form of clutter that you need to get rid of as a minimalist is the material possessions that take up too much space in your home. However, you should also learn how to get rid of emotional clutter, as this can compromise your peace of mind. While you may find decluttering material possessions an easy task, getting rid of your emotional baggage

51

is a different story. This is a challenging task but it isn't impossible.

To get rid of our emotional clutter, you should try to remind yourself that you are creating a strong family with the most wonderful people in the world. Do this each day. No matter what happened to you in the past, you are now in the presence of people who love you unconditionally and will always support you no matter what. If there have been people or instances that have hurt you in the past, learn how to let go of these one by one. Create a list of the things that bring you negative emotions and work on letting them go. Do this by creating another list, this time of the good things and the good people (especially your family) in your life right now.

Combat your emotional clutter with love and positivity. If you need to, ask help from your spouse, your parents or your children. Writing the good things down and reminding yourself of these on a daily basis will show you what a beautiful life you have right now and how you shouldn't hang on to the past, especially if you want to become a minimalist at heart.

- **Practice 3: Own your relationships**

   Finally, learn how to own your relationships and keep them as your own. This final practice is quite challenging as you need to learn how to become fully present and aware of your family values. These days, it's so easy to be influenced by social media, influencers, and other people who want to deprive you of happiness, whether intentionally or not. Sadly, this is how the modern-day world works and there isn't anything you can do to change it.

   But what you *can* change are your relationships with the members of your family. To avoid the dangers of losing your relationships to the complexity of the world, make sure you keep them to yourself. When it comes to your relationships, this is when you can be greedy. For instance, if people want you to share things about your family, don't give away too much. Don't share too much about your personal life and that of your family. This is especially true for any issues that you have dealt with personally or as a family. If you really want to share your family experiences with others, just share what you, and the members of your family, feel comfortable with. If things start feeling weird, stop.

For this practice, incorporate authenticity and mindfulness so that you can realize the impact of the outside world on your relationships. If you think that your relationships have turned sour because of these effects, take the necessary steps to change them. Just remain true to yourself and, hopefully, the rest of your family will follow.

As you can see, when it comes to minimalism and family, authenticity is the most important thing. Society will place a lot of pressure on you and your relationships so you should have the strength to fight these off and keep your family protected. This is part of your journey towards minimalism and it will surely change your life for the better.

CHAPTER 5:

THE POWER OF DOING VERSUS HAVING

When you have less, you can do more.

Doing is a powerful thing as it allows you to initiate changes in your life that you never thought were possible in the past. But it's virtually impossible to do something as a family when even just one member of the group is unwilling to participate. In this case, if you want to adopt a minimalist lifestyle and one member of your family blatantly refuses to take part in this endeavor. However, if you manage to convince your entire family of the benefits of minimalism and they are all ready to let go of unnecessary things, this is when you will be able to do more for your own empowerment.

Let's start this chapter off with an exercise: try to think of one significant change you made in your life. What process did you go through to achieve this? For me, whenever I want to make a change in my life, I always start by planning. For instance, a few years ago, I decided to start the Mediterranean diet. Before I started following the diet, I did research about it. I educated myself about the diet and I even spoke to my doctor about it. Then I came up with a plan for how to follow it, like what foods I would eliminate first, how long I would wait before eliminating another type of food, and so on. I literally created a plan to follow from the very beginning. When I had everything ready, I executed my plan. And now, I am happy with how the Mediterranean diet improved my health, and it has now become a part of my life.

In this example from my life, the most important step I took to change my diet is the execution of my plan. I didn't stop at planning. I took action, and this was when I was able to make the switch from a traditional diet to a more specialized one. In the same way, when you create your own plan for becoming a minimalist, the most important thing for you to do is take action. Doing is truly a powerful thing as it has the potential to initiate change and make things better for yourself and your family.

All About Having

Today's world is all about having. People want to have the latest gadgets, the most expensive cars, the biggest houses, and other extravagant things to show off to the world even if, most of the time, they cannot even afford these things. This is the main focus of the culture of consumerism and it is what makes a lot of people feel miserable with their lives.

Unfortunately, consumerism is powerful. Once you get hooked, it becomes very difficult to envision yourself living a simple life. Therefore, the more you have, the more you will want. And the more you want, the more you will focus on material things instead of the people you share your life and your home with. Instead of doing something to change your life, you will only focus on having things so people will be impressed with you and see you as someone who matters. Then again, when this is your focus... how will you be true to yourself?

Just like minimalism, consumerism is also a concept that has been around for a long time now. However, this concept is the exact opposite of minimalism as it encourages you to acquire, collect, and showcase material things instead of trimming things down to the basics. Consumerism is a dangerous concept as it can potentially end up getting you addicted to spending more than you can afford. It won't just affect your finances, but it will also have a negative effect on your well-being.

When you have a powerful urge to have, this leads to a more stressful life. You work hard to pay your bills but as soon as your money comes, you spend it on other things—on things that you feel you must have right away. Then you remember that your bills are left unpaid and you've spent the money you need to support your family. In such a case, you might end up taking a loan or borrowing money from lending institutions just to get by. Then the items that you spent your hard-earned money on end up as part of the clutter in your home. If this keeps happening, you will eventually find yourself in a tight spot, which, in turn, will make you feel incredibly stressed.

Is this kind of stress really worth the thrill of having things that you don't really need? And the sad part is, the thrill you get from purchasing all those things won't last long. Eventually, you will forget the good feelings, and then you will start focusing on the next things that you want to have. This creates a vicious cycle that may start eating at your life and the relationships you have with your family. But if you focus on the more important things in your life like your family, you won't have to go through this never-ending destructive cycle of consumerism.

As a minimalist, having material things shouldn't matter to you. Unless you want to have more space, more time with your family, and more happiness, having shouldn't be your focus. Beyond your efforts to lessen your material possessions and avoid purchasing more things than you need or can afford, minimalism has a deeper purpose. One of the more profound things that can happen to you when you pursue minimalism is being able to find more meaning in your life. Through minimalism, you can focus on intangible things that money can't buy, but are far more valuable to your life. The idea behind minimalism is that when you're able to get rid of material things that you don't need, you can find the things that bring you deep joy.

As part of your journey, it's time to stop focusing on having. Instead, use minimalism as a tool to help you find freedom from consumerism and the obsession to own too many material things. This will bring you peace along with a wonderful sense of freedom from guilt, anxiety, and the chains of modern society that keep us focused on living a life that we don't really want for ourselves.

Learning How to Let Go

One of the key concepts behind minimalism is learning how to let go of the things that you don't need so you can do more with your family and the other people in your life. Letting go also happens to be the main thing you can do to counteract the power of having. When you learn to let go, the urge to have more things fades away. When you let go of the things that don't matter, you will have time to bond with your family, spend time in the great outdoors, go for a walk or a run, and do other things that you were too busy for when you were focused on material things. As an individual and a member of your family, the power of doing versus having is one of the most significant lessons you have to learn.

Buying new things even if you don't need them is caused by the power of having. On the contrary, letting go of the things that aren't essential to your life is fueled by the power of doing. The mere act of letting go is already a huge step towards becoming a minimalist. But before you can start decluttering your life by letting things go, you must first have the willingness to do so. Minimalism encourages you to let go of anything superfluous, excessive, and unnecessary. And you can start the process by searching for the things in your home that have already gathered a thick layer of dust because you haven't used or even touched them since you left them there.

However, there are certain material possessions we own that are just too difficult to let go of. Although the ultimate goal of minimalism is to let go of the things you don't need, this doesn't mean that you should learn this right away. For you to accept the fact that letting go is part of this lifestyle, don't be too hard on yourself. For instance, if you really can't let go of an item of clothing, a decorative piece, or any other thing, don't force yourself to get rid of it. Give yourself time to accept the process of letting go and it will, eventually, become easier. Usually, the instances that make it difficult for you to let things go are:

- When you feel guilty because someone important to you gave you the item even though you don't really like it or you haven't even used it since you received it.
- When the item has sentimental value to you, or it is associated with some important memories.
- When you really believe that you might still need or use the item even though it has been sitting in storage for as long as you can remember.
- When you have decluttered one room of your home, and you feel like it's too empty, thus, you're finding it difficult to do the same thing with the other rooms.

These are some of the most common reasons why people find it too difficult to let things go. But, as I have mentioned several times throughout this book, letting go is a crucial aspect of minimalism. So, to help you out, here are some tips and ideas for you to ponder on about the art of letting go:

1. **Accept that nothing is permanent**

   This is a very common concept, although a lot of people either forget or ignore it. In this world, nothing is permanent. Seasons change, friends come and go, items get worn out, and we all grow old. If you can accept this fact, it becomes easier for you to let things go. As you sit in a room with the intent to declutter, keep this in your mind. This will make it easier for you to let things go instead of keeping them "just in case."

2. **Learn from your mistakes**

   When you look at all the things you own, you may realize that a lot of those things were purchased on impulse. But once you have brought these items home, you realize that you don't really need them and so you keep them in storage for situations when you will need them. But such situations don't usually come. Since these items are already in your possession, accept them and learn from your mistakes. The next time you are faced with situations where you want to buy something, think carefully before you take out your wallet and pay for these items.

3. Define what is important to you

Your material possessions shouldn't define you. Once you can accept this fact, it becomes easier to let things go. Material possessions shouldn't define you. These possessions shouldn't replace your relationships either. The most important things in life cannot be bought, and these are the ones that will make your life more fulfilling. Try to make a list of things that add authentic value to your life. Make sure that your list doesn't contain any material things. Writing these things down makes it easier to let things go because you have defined the things that are deeply important to you.

4. Intentionally break your chain of materialism

If you remember, one of the core concepts behind minimalism is intentionality. Just like doing, intentionality is a powerful thing and you should use this to break your chain of materialism. When faced with the choice to purchase material things, awaken your intentionality to help you avoid giving in to your impulses. This is one thing that you may need to practice on, but over time, it will become easier. And this intentionality won't make you feel anxious about letting things go.

5. Gain more out of less

Finally, when you realize that you will actually gain more by letting go, this makes things easier for you too. Yes, it will be difficult at the beginning. But the more you practice the act of letting go, the easier it becomes. And when you start experiencing the wonderful benefits of letting go, this will inspire you to keep going. As a minimalist, letting go helps you realize what's truly important in life. If you can convince the rest of your family to do the same, then you can all work together to make minimalism your way of life.

Practicing the Power of Doing Versus Having

Practicing doing versus having is a skill which means that you can gain mastery of this the more you do it. To practice 'doing,' all you have to do is learn how to enjoy doing things that don't require the use of material things and do these things regularly. Learn to appreciate the simple, fun, and material-free activities rather than focusing on activities that require too many things or too much money. Then rope your family into these activities so you can spend quality time having fun together while learning how to appreciate each other without the need for material things. There are so many things you can do to help you appreciate the pleasure of doing. Here are some examples:

- Rather than purchasing something new for yourself or for one of the members of your family, find something in your room and donate it. Do this regularly and it will surely make you feel better about yourself. As a parent, you can either look for an item of clothing, a decorative item, or even something from your kitchen and give it to charity. You can also encourage your children to do this: ask them to choose one of their toys or books to give away and let them be the one to give the item they have chosen for them to experience the act of giving.

- When it's time to create a shopping list, just write everything that comes to mind. But before you go out to shop, take some time to sit down and go through the list you have created. Try to determine if there are any items in your list that you can actually remove or reduce the quantity of. For instance, if you're writing a grocery list and you planned to purchase a dozen pack of cookies, you may reduce this to half a dozen. Or if you have planned your meals for the week and you discover that the ingredients you have included in your list are excessive, remove some of the items or reduce them so you don't end up buying more than you need. Do this every time you create a shopping list and you can save a lot of money and time in the long-run.

- Encourage your family to join you in fun activities that don't involve spending money or using material things like going to the park, hiking, having your own sports fest, having a "cooking class" at home, and more. There are so many family activities that you can do to have fun, strengthen your bonds, and spend quality time with each other. The time you spend together is important as it makes you realize what wonderful people the members of your family are.

Minimalism doesn't have to be out-of-reach just because your family consists of people with different personalities. When you think about it, families will always have something in common. As long as you know that thing that you share as a family, you can encourage them to join you in your quest to becoming a minimalist. Share with them the benefits of minimalism and show them how they can adopt this simple lifestyle in small yet significant ways. Aside from doing things with your family, you can share with them some of the most important concepts of minimalism to help them understand what this movement, lifestyle, and concept is all about. Here are some things you can share with your family about minimalism:

- You don't have to live your life just like everyone else. Your family is unique. You should find your own sweet spot to help you accept minimalism willingly without developing any negative feelings toward each other.
- You don't need material things to live a full and happy life. Instead, you should focus on your family to strengthen your bonds and make it easier for you to transition to living a life with less.

- You should learn how to live within your means. This is something that can significantly help you become a family of minimalists. If you don't need something or you cannot afford it, don't buy it anymore. It's better to live a life of less than to live a life worrying about the debts you have to pay because you choose to live extravagantly.

- Try to practice sharing with others. This is one activity you can do that can make it easier for you to appreciate what you have. When you expose yourself to other people, especially the ones who are in need, this will make you realize how lucky you are with what you have and with the people you share your life with.

Finally, all the activities you do and the efforts you put into becoming a minimalist should show you and your family the importance of focusing on your relationships. Even if you are raising young children, practicing minimalism is entirely possible. All you have to do is set your mind to it and start taking the necessary steps to live a simpler and more enriching life.

CHAPTER 6:

LESS STUFF, MORE BLISS

Ultimately, one of the things you want to get out of your new lifestyle is to become happier. The less stuff you have, the more blissful you can become. By letting go of all that is unnecessary, you will find more bliss and joy in the few material possessions that you have because they don't distract you from the many intangible things that you need in your life.

In this chapter, you will learn the things to do so you can become a better 'declutterer' and a more effective minimalist. As long as you are willing to embrace the "less is more" way of life, you can start your journey towards true minimalism. In fact, you can even think of it this way: when you have less stuff to worry about, you have more of a life to live. As a minimalist myself, this is one thing that I can attest to. Since I started embracing the minimalist way of life, I have seen so many improvements in myself and my whole family.

Minimalism is a way to detox your life just like you would eat healthier foods to detox your body and become healthier. Minimal living is being able to live with less stuff so you can make space for more. Here are a few benefits that show you how blissful your life can be through minimalism:

- You don't need to spend a lot of effort and time cleaning your home because there isn't much to clean. This means that you can focus on doing other chores that you might have neglected in the past.

- You don't need to spend your money on unnecessary stuff. Instead, you can spend on things like travel, healthy food, and other things that you and your family need to lead better, happier lives.

- You don't need to spend so much time choosing what to wear each morning, what car to use to go to work, and so on. Basically, your life becomes simpler because you don't have so many things to choose from every time you need to do something.

- You don't need to feel stressed because there is so much clutter in your home. Clutter can make you feel anxious, it can take up your brain space, and it can cause problems in your family. But without clutter, you don't have to feel all of these things. Instead, you can bask in the cleanliness and spaciousness of your room while spending quality time with the members of your family.

And one of the best things that can come out of choosing to live minimally is that once you make the decision and you take the first steps, you will feel like a heavy weight has been lifted off your shoulders. When you realize that you don't have to give in to the pressures of society and you don't have to keep spending your money on things that you don't need, this immediately makes you feel better about your life. This decision also comes with a sense of empowerment as you walk through different malls and shops without feeling the need to buy something before walking out. This is one of the most freeing feelings I have ever experienced in my life, and you can feel it too.

When You Just Can't Have Enough

No matter where you are from, you may have already been influenced by the culture of wanting to collect material things. This is a very powerful culture that has affected the actions and decisions of people. For instance, when one person has one bank account and one credit card, they open another bank account so they can apply for another credit card. While having one credit card works just fine, there's just something appealing with having more than one of these plastic cards in their wallet. Or if someone owns a car that works just fine, they still feel the need to purchase another car to fill up the empty space in the garage. These are some common examples of how the modern-day culture has influenced the actions of people pushing them to keep buying things to make their lives seem fuller.

These days, people value material possessions more than their relationships, their health, and even a meaningful life. Because of this line of thinking, people who already struggle with their finances keep living a lifestyle that they cannot afford because they are only focused on having instead of doing. Sadly though, they don't experience true bliss by living this kind of life. In fact, it's often the opposite as they may feel stressed as they try to cope with all the pressures and expectations of the material-centered culture.

Trying to pursue material possessions will never make you truly happy. This is a fact. Think about the people who own a dozen cars, enormous mansions, closets full of clothes, and other extravagant things. At the end of the day, they always feel like something is missing in their lives. They keep purchasing more things to try and fill this void. If you allow yourself to fall into this trap, you might never find the happiness you are yearning to have. And this applies to everyone who gets obsessed with material things. Let's take a look at what may happen to you when you just can't seem to have enough:

1. The more you have, the more you want

Have you ever seen a child open presents on their birthday? Usually, children would open one present, feel momentary happiness because of the present, then toss it aside and move on to the next one. This might seem silly to a lot of people but this is how adults are too. For instance, if a person is obsessed with gadgets, they would do everything they can to get the newest model as soon as it comes out. Once the person has it,

65

they would feel the thrill for a couple of days as they learn more about their new gadget. But after a few days, life goes on until news of the next new model comes out.

When you have an obsession with having things, it will never be enough. The more things you have, the more you will want to have things. Then you will be stuck in an endless loop of hoping, spending, and having. And while you are focusing on your material possessions, life is already passing you by.

2. You will be so busy using, maintaining, or thinking about your possessions

With all the gadgets, appliances, and equipment you buy, you won't have time to focus on anything else. You will just be using the newly purchased gadgets, maintaining the new vehicles that you brought home, and thinking about other things that you wish you had. All of these actions will occupy your time, your attention, and sometimes even your love. This is one of the most common effects that will directly affect the relationships you have with the members of your family.

3. The more stuff you have, the more clutter your home will have

When you buy new things, they will always end up in your home. From furniture to gadgets, appliances, clothes, and more, you will be bringing home all of these material possessions. Then you would have to find places for all these things inside your home. Eventually, you will run out of storage space. And when this happens, all of these items end up as clutter, which, in turn, adds to the stress in your life.

4. There will always be something to distract you

When it comes to material possessions, it's impossible to give them up unless you make an intentional choice to do so. This is because manufacturers, businesses, and suppliers will always find ways to make new things for people to buy. Whether it would be a cellphone, a game console, toys, appliances, or accessories, there are endless ideas out there and you just cannot tell them to stop making new things so that you stop buying them.

If you want to break your habit of collecting material things, you have to make a conscious decision to do this, then take the necessary steps to help you eliminate this habit from your life. Otherwise, these things will just continue to distract you from the more important things in your life.

The saddest thing about always wanting more is that at the end of the day, you realize that people won't really feel impressed with everything you have collected throughout the years. And no matter how many possessions you have, no matter how much clutter you have in your home, there will always be other people who have more. If you want to free yourself of this feeling, you can do so by setting your intention of becoming a minimalist.

The Beauty of Decluttering

On your path towards becoming a minimalist, one of the most significant things you can do is learn how to declutter correctly. Decluttering is a process where you get rid of unnecessary things while keeping everything that you need in your life. By now, you should have already accepted the "less is more" concept. To achieve this, decluttering is key. Also, by now, you already know that you would only have to get rid of things that you don't absolutely need or the ones that don't add value to your life. It's important to accept and understand that when you start living with less, bliss will soon follow.

Once you realize that you already have less and that you have broken free of the chains of materialism, you will feel even more content. The freedom you will feel as a minimalist comes when your home has been decluttered down to the bare necessities. When this happens, you will be able to see the people sharing your home with you—your family—and you won't feel like you need anything else.

While decluttering may seem like a simple task, it isn't. Decluttering isn't just about throwing things away to rid your home of your possessions so that you can call it a day and claim that you are a minimalist. Instead, decluttering involves intentionality, focus, and a lot of self-reflection. You cannot just go around your house picking up everything that's on the shelves or the floor then simply putting in the trash. If this is how you declutter your home, you will end up with a lot of negative feelings, especially coming from the members of your family.

To use decluttering to minimize your life, you must learn how to do it correctly. A minimalist home isn't something that is devoid of life. You shouldn't tell your family that you are decluttering, then take all of their possessions and throw them away. Consider the feelings of your family members, as well as your own feelings, when you go through your material possessions to determine what to keep and what to get rid of.

The great thing about decluttering is that it doesn't need to be a difficult experience. Although this process isn't simple, you don't have to see it as a negative thing. For instance, if you plan to declutter your closet and donate all the items of clothing that you don't want or need anymore, think about the people you will be helping. Instead of leaving your clothes to sit in your room, gathering dust and mold, you can provide other people with clothing so they don't freeze out there in the cold. Also, you don't have to declutter your home in a single day. This is a process that takes time, and you should relish the time it takes to clear your home of unnecessary things. To help you look forward to this important step in minimalism, here are some reasons why decluttering is a beautiful thing:

- **Decluttering helps you determine what is important to you**

  When you're immersed in the process of decluttering, you are forced to reflect on the things that you own. In the past, you might have found it difficult to let go of things. But when you intentionally start decluttering, you will also start thinking about everything that you own, thus, allowing you to determine what to keep and what to give away. Through this process, you will find out what matters to you.

- **Decluttering provides you with emotional relief**

There is nothing like the feeling you get after you have decluttered an entire room in your home. For me, I started with my study, and I was able to get rid of so much stuff that I realized wasn't really important. After I decluttered my study (it took one whole week), I looked around the room and realized how beautiful it was. Prior to decluttering, I always felt that my study was so messy and it caused me stress. But after working on that room, it became one of my favorite rooms in the house.

In line with this, decluttering gives you an opportunity to get rid of items that come with negative emotions. If there are things you own that remind you of painful or unpleasant memories from the past, decluttering gives you a reason to finally let these things go. This is another part of the process that provides you with a lot of emotional relief.

- **Decluttering frees up a lot of space in your home**

This is the more obvious result of your decluttering efforts. The more you get rid of things, the more space you will have in your home. Whether you have a large home or a small one, decluttering will make you realize that you actually have more space than you need. And with this newfound space, you and your family can interact more freely as you don't have to bump into things all the time or end up fighting with each other because of things that you can't find as they get lost in the clutter.

- **Decluttering saves you money**

  When you declutter, you will discover things that you forgot you had. For instance, if you wanted to purchase a new set of plates because the set you're using has already become worn-out and chipped in several places, you might discover that you actually have a new set of plates or two stored away in your kitchen cupboard. This happens when you buy things that you don't need—you end up putting them away because the items you're currently using are still functional.

  When you find such things in your home, this means that you don't have to spend your hard-earned money to buy replacements for broken, damaged, or old items. You can even organize a garage sale so you can sell everything that you have decided to get rid of. Although you won't get back all the money you spent on these items, you will still have some return on investment that you can put into your savings or your emergency fund.

The beauty of decluttering is that it sets you free. No longer do you have to be defined by your material possessions as you will be getting rid of these little by little. And the more you declutter your home, the closer you get to having a simple, functional home to house your minimalist family.

How to Declutter

Although decluttering is an important part of minimalism, I am not saying that this is an easy process. If you have never let go of any of your material possessions before, getting rid of most of these items (which you will be doing when you declutter your home) will seem like a mammoth task. After all, each time you have purchased these items, you convinced yourself that you could not live without those things. Therefore, if you decide to let these things go, it will definitely make you feel anxious or apprehensive.

Don't worry, we have all been there. We have all experienced those same feelings at the beginning of our journey, but we powered through them by reminding ourselves that less is more and less stuff means more bliss in life. To help make decluttering easier for you, here are some steps to guide you:

1. **Learn how to work smarter not harder**

   Working harder isn't always the solution to life's problems. When it comes to decluttering, working smarter pays off more than working harder. This just means that coming up with a plan or a strategy to declutter your home in the most organized way will help you achieve your goals faster than if you merely force yourself to declutter non-stop without thinking about the things you want to keep and the things you want to get rid of. Decluttering is a task that requires self-reflection. Without it, this process loses its meaning and it won't help towards your main goal of becoming a minimalist.

2. **If you don't use it, let it go**

   I cannot stress this point enough. When you come across objects that you don't use anymore or you haven't used since you bought them, this makes them unnecessary. And when you find unnecessary things in your home, learn how to let them go. Stop trying to convince yourself that you will use these items in the near future when they have been gathering dust for the past few years. You know the kind of life you lead; therefore, you should know whether or not material things bring meaning to your life. This may be difficult at first but it will get easier the more you practice letting things go.

3. **Learn how to live with a smaller wardrobe**

   If you own a closet full of clothes, you would have already experienced the problem of not being able to decide what to wear. When you have too many clothes, it becomes very difficult to make this choice. Even if your closet is brimming with clothes, you still feel like you have nothing to wear. If you want to get rid of this problem, declutter your closet too.

Have you ever heard of the 333 Project? This is where you would only wear 33 items of clothing for three months. This could be great practice for you before you start decluttering your closet. Pick a range of clothing items for your closet until you have 33 pieces. Place these in a separate container, and for the next three months, just choose clothes from that selection. I have personally tried this and found that it is very effective. After three months, it was also easier for me to declutter my closet and let go of clothes that I know I won't ever use again.

4. **Extend your minimalism to other tasks such as reading and writing**

If you focus too much on decluttering, you might eventually get tired of it. To avoid this, you can practice minimalism in other ways. For instance, you can read some books on minimalism (just like this one) and write down the events of your minimalist journey in a journal. As you do these activities, intentionally try to slow down. Focus on what you are doing and this will help improve your agility too. Doing activities like these will help you feel refreshed so that you can go back to the task of decluttering feeling more motivated and inspired.

5. **Focus on whole, healthy foods to keep you nourished on your journey**

Along the same lines as taking a break from decluttering, make sure that you are nourishing your body properly by eating the healthiest foods. Remember that minimalism in itself is already a huge change to make in your life. At some point, you may feel frustrated, hesitant, and you might even want to give up when things get very challenging, especially when dealing with your family.

When you end up becoming physically ill because of the stress you're feeling, this will add to your negativity. Avoid this by making sure that everything you eat and everything you feed to your family will provide the right kind of nourishment while making your body strong enough to handle all the challenges that come your way.

6. Think about what is essential in your life

This particular tip will help make decluttering easier for you. When you reflect on the things that are essential in your life, you won't have to spend too much time deciding whether to keep certain things or not. If you think that it will help, create a list of priorities and use this list as your basis for when you are decluttering the rooms of your home. This eliminates the uncertainty from the process, thus, making it more manageable for you and your family.

7. Other creative decluttering pointers for you

Since decluttering is an essential aspect of minimalism, it is something that you will have to do at one point or another. Don't fight it. Accept it and think of it as one of the most significant steps you will take to become a true minimalist. Here are a few more creative tips to inspire you:

o Start the habit of decluttering by spending five to 10 minutes each day on the task. This is especially important if it is your first time trying decluttering. This time period may seem short, but as long as you are fully intent on using those precious minutes to declutter, you can make progress.
o When you're already used to decluttering, fill a whole trash bag each time you declutter a space in your home. Then either throw out or donate everything in the trash bag without looking back.
o Create a checklist to help you declutter your whole house in an organized way. Start by making a list of all the rooms you plan to declutter and each time you accomplish a task,

cross it out or place a checkmark next to it.

- o Find one item in your home each day that you will donate to someone in need. If you really do this each day, that means you would have given away 365 items throughout the year!

- o Give the 12-12-12 Challenge a try. For this, find 12 items in your home to donate, 12 items to throw out, and 12 items to keep. Just make sure that the items you keep are truly essential.

- o Take before and after photos of all the rooms in your home so you can keep track of the progress you are making. By the end of the process, you will have a collection of photos that feature clean, relaxing, and clutter-free rooms.

Finally, don't do this task on your own. While you may start decluttering by yourself, show your family how beneficial it is to do so and how good this process makes you feel. Then you can encourage them to join in, especially when it's time to start working on their own rooms or in the common rooms in your home. When you work together, decluttering becomes easier, faster, and more fun.

CHAPTER 7:

MINIMALISM FOR PARENTS

As a parent, encouraging your children to adopt minimalism might not be such an easy task, especially if they grew up in the same culture where material possessions are valued over anything else. But if you want your whole family to improve through minimalism, it's essential for you to learn how to get your children on board. Forget about forcing them to adopt minimalism as this will only make it a negative thing for them. Instead, it's better to focus on showing them why minimalism is great and how it doesn't have to feel like they are sacrificing things or throwing things away just for the sake of it.

Whether you are a new parent or you have already been in the parenting game for some time now, applying minimalism to parenthood comes with its own unique set of challenges. But just like any other changes in life, when you can overcome these challenges, you come out as a stronger parent with children who understand what minimalism means and are willing to simplify their lives for the better.

It seems like parenting these days is much more complicated than it was in the past. You may still remember how your parents raised you, and when you try to compare their parenting style with yours, you will realize how much things have changed. In the past, it was okay for parents to be strict with their children. Now, when you do this, especially in public, you may be seen as the enemy. Being a parent these days may also mean that you are always in competition with other parents, you are more fearful about the safety of your children, and there is always the idea that if you buy a lot of stuff for your child, this is considered as a parenting win.

But as a minimalist parent, you want to avoid buying too many things for your child all the time. You want to focus on teaching your children what really matters in life beyond material possessions. Of course, the best way to teach this to your children is to show them that you are willing or even excited to become a minimalist. The more you show your authenticity in terms of adopting minimalism, the more they will see how important this lifestyle is and how it can benefit their lives in different ways.

When teaching minimalism to your children, this shouldn't just be about material possessions. You should also encourage them to find the simple joys in life, and this can only happen if you don't push them into things that they don't want to do. For instance, these days, there are so many children who have full schedules from ballet lessons, music lessons, swimming lessons, and more. While all of these are great activities, filling your child's schedule from morning until night can be extremely exhausting for them. Also, they won't even have time to play or spend time with you. To become a great minimalist parent, you should try to find the perfect balance between having fun and teaching responsibilities to your children. And this will be our main focus throughout this chapter.

The Stress of Modern-Day Parenting

As a parent, you are faced with just as much adversity as your children. For most parents, having a child and raising that child are the most important missions we have in life. However, in a fast-paced world that's based on material possessions, competition, and heartbreak, raising a child can be extremely stressful. A lot of times, people talk about how children often disappoint their parents. This is a common thing, and it is expected. But when parents are the ones who fail their children, whether intentionally or not, it doesn't affect them as much.

This is because children these days aren't focused on their parents. Since they are given so many things, they grow up without placing much value on their relationships.

Raising a child isn't an easy task, especially if you don't have the resources for it. Despite this, a lot of parents still go above and beyond when it comes to buying things for their children. They do this to compete with other parents, compensate for their failures, or just to make their children happy. But when it comes to the happiness of your children, should you rely on material things?

As you are learning to become a minimalist, you should know that the answer to that question is, no. You want to live a minimalist lifestyle to improve your life and your relationships with your family. Therefore, if you are currently raising a child too, you should start teaching them the value of minimalism early on.

Modern-day parenting is exceptionally challenging because the world is too focused on material things. And if you can't afford it, this makes you look bad. Even if you don't care, your children might feel bad when they realize that they don't own as much stuff as their peers. As a minimalist parent, it is your responsibility to instill the values of minimalism in your child. If they give in to pressure from other people, you will end up having a lot of arguments with your children. For instance, if other children at school are always bragging about the new things their parents bought for them and your child cannot brag because you don't buy them anything on a regular basis, this might make them feel bad. If they don't understand minimalism and they don't accept it, being a minimalist parent becomes even more difficult.

On the other hand, if you can successfully raise your child as a minimalist, they won't care what other people think. They will listen to other children brag, feel good about the happiness those other children are feeling, and still remain grateful for their own situation because they know that they belong to a loving family where the main priority is each other. If you can raise such a child, you won't feel stressed about being a minimalist parent. At the end of the day, it's all about sticking with your beliefs and trying your best to raise your children with the same set of beliefs. Don't force them into it. Nurture them, respect them, and show them the love they deserve. These are the best strategies you can employ to help your children understand the value of minimalism, so they make it their own way of life too.

Applying Minimalism to Your Family's Life

Once you apply minimalism to your life as a parent and you start applying it to your children's lives too, this is an excellent way for you to handle challenges that come your way. Minimalism brings you closer as a family; therefore, the more you practice it, the stronger your bonds become. And the best part is, there are so many practical things you can do to bring minimalism to your family. Here are a few ways to apply minimalism to your family's life:

1. **Never stop organizing things**

   Even after you have decluttered all of the rooms in your home, your job isn't done yet. In fact, your job as a parent will never be done because organization is an unending cycle. As a parent, if you want minimalism to become a permanent part of your life, you must work to keep it that way. Imagine what would happen if everyone in your family puts in the effort to declutter and organize the whole home. Then once that's done, you all go back to your old ways. In a month or two, you might discover that your home has been invaded by clutter once again.

   Don't let this happen! Make sure that things stay organized by setting your own daily routines then teaching your children to have these daily minimalist routines too. For instance, before going to bed, you can go through the whole house to check if any clutter is building up in any rooms, spaces, or surfaces. You can teach your children to do this night time checking in their own rooms while you check the rest of the house. This is an easy way to spot things that don't belong and avoid clutter from coming back. Building routines also solidifies minimalism as your lifestyle instead of a passing fad that you just tried out.

2. Start small

If this is the first time that you introduce minimalism to your children, start small. Don't overwhelm them by asking them to help you declutter the biggest room in your home. Instead, you can start by focusing on a small area where your child's personal possessions are. Go through their items one at a time and talk to your children throughout the process. In doing this, you are showing your children that you're willing to put in the work along with them, and you also respect them enough to ask for their opinions about their own things instead of just throwing everything out.

3. Sort through your children's wardrobe too

I have already shared some tips about minimizing your wardrobe to make things simpler for you. This is an excellent tip because it works with people of all ages. Even while your children are young, you can train them to feel satisfied with a small wardrobe. That way, you can trust them to make decisions in terms of choosing their own attire each day, and when they grow up, you don't have to worry that your children will keep asking you for money just to buy new clothes. This tip saves time, money, and the stress of having to argue with a teenager about how they don't need new clothes when they have a closet full of clothes to choose from.

4. Get rid of things that don't hold significance

Just as you would think about the significance of each item before throwing it, encourage your children to do some self-reflection while you are decluttering with them. Whether the items in question are toys, craft supplies, decorative items, or anything else, ask your children if these items are significant to them. Remember the tip about asking difficult questions? You can do that here. Help your child make important decisions by asking them questions that will help them determine the true significance of their personal belongings. If they realize that some of the items don't actually hold any significance, these are the items that you can encourage them to get rid of.

5. **Avoid "shopping for the future"**

These days, there are so many parents who fall into the trap of shopping for the future. For instance, if your 5-year-old son is currently crazy about everything dinosaurs, you would try looking for dinosaur-themed items to please them. Then as you are shopping, you come across a beautiful attire that also happens to be three sizes too big for your son. Since you know how much your little boy loves dinosaurs, you purchase the attire anyway so you can give it to them in the future.

But what if your son isn't into dinosaurs anymore by the time the attire already fits him? What then? This is an example of how some parents think that they are making a good purchase when, in fact, they have only spent their hard-earned money on something that becomes part of the clutter in their home. Avoid falling into the same trap by only buying things that you and your children need right now. When the future comes, that is when you should shop for your future needs. Although planning for the future is a good idea, this doesn't apply to buying things and storing them, especially if you want to become a family of minimalists.

6. **Be aware of paper clutter**

As children grow into toddlers and they discover how much fun it is to draw, cut, color, and scribble on paper, there will be this stage where they just want to work with paper constantly. Whether at home or in school, your children will create these precious projects that you just can throw away. However, all of these projects made of paper can add up quickly, and if you just keep collecting them, you will end up having endless piles and stacks of paper clutter.

Of course, I am not saying that you should ask your child to throw away their projects after you've seen them. It's okay to accept these artworks, store them for up to a week, then either recycle or reuse them regularly. It's your job to sort through the paper clutter and only keep the best ones. What I do with my boys is to take a picture of each of their artworks. Then, we create beautiful digital albums of their artwork together. We keep the original of only their few favorites and alternate them in a magnetic frame on the fridge.

As a parent, applying minimalism to your family's life involves encouraging them to join you in your journey. Although this may take time, be patient with them. Just keep showing them how much minimalism can improve your lives and try not to make it seem like a negative thing in any way. This becomes easier if you yourself believe that minimalism is a good thing, and you know that it will change your life for the better.

Minimalism for Parents With Babies and Toddlers

If you want to become a great minimalist parent for your baby or toddler, start by living with less. Today, children need minimalism more than ever. All of the material possessions that surround children make them lose focus. They become so used to chaos that they start believing that chaos is what life is all about. This shouldn't be the case, especially if minimalism will be your way of life. When you have an infant or toddler to raise, here are some tips to guide you:

1. **Take the time to show your little ones what minimalism is all about**

    For you to successfully teach minimalism to young children, you need to take the time for it. Unlike your spouse or a teenager, you cannot just sit your child down and explain what minimalism is. With young children, it's all about demonstrating what is right and doing the same things again and again until they really learn those things. Teaching minimalism to children takes a lot of time and patience, but all of your efforts will pay off in the end as you will successfully raise a minimalist child.

2. Give your children freedom

While it is your responsibility as a parent to protect your children, this doesn't mean that you shouldn't give them the freedom to live their lives and experience different things. As long as you are around to supervise your children and make sure that their lives aren't threatened, loosen the reigns a bit. Allow your child to take risks. If they fall or hurt themselves, explain why this happened. When teaching your child about minimalism by getting rid of certain things, allow them to choose which one to keep and which one to let go. When you give your children choices and the freedom to make those choices, they grow up with self-confidence and stronger values.

3. Don't try to keep your children entertained all the time

These days, it's very common to see children spending hours and hours in front of televisions, tablets, and other electronic gadgets. It seems like parents these days are so afraid of what might happen if they don't keep their children entertained by these screens all the time. If you're one such parent, try to take away those screens and allow your children to interact with other children. Allow them to play outside, run, jump, and enjoy physical games with others.

Try not to worry about keeping your children entertained all the time. The great thing about children is that when you let them be, they will always find things to do because to them, the world is a magical place filled with potential. And this is an excellent way to view the world, especially if you want to raise your child as a minimalist.

4. Teach your children to be responsible

Minimalism is all about being responsible for yourself. It's about sticking with your values even though other people don't agree with you. One way to teach this to your child is to teach them how to be responsible even at a young age. To do this, try not to control their lives too much. Avoid creating rigid schedules that they must adhere to. Otherwise, they might get used to simply following others instead of making their own choices. Create a routine for them but allow for some flexibility.

If they want to mix things up, let them. As long as they do all the things on the list, they would have completed their nighttime routine. This teaches your children to be responsible for their own actions without having to force them to follow strict rules or schedules.

5. **Make things fun for your children**

The most effective way to teach new things to children is by making the learning process fun. And when it comes to teaching minimalism, you can do this in so many ways. For instance, when teaching children to tidy up their room or play area, sing a song while doing it. You can either create your own silly song or download one online. Listening to music and singing while doing a seemingly boring task makes it more fun.

Or when you're trying to convince your child to get rid of some of their toys. Instead of forcing them to choose what to give up, you can make a game out of it. You can also think of a story where there are children who have no toys to play with, and since your child has a lot, sharing one or two of their toys would mean the world to those who have none. It's all about making things more enjoyable for your children, especially for babies and toddlers who love to play and have fun.

6. **Practice flexibility while remaining practical**

When you're thinking of ways to encourage your young children to adopt minimalism into their lives, try to be as practical as possible. There is no need for you to think of elaborate schemes that you might not be able to pull off because they are too complex. Instead, think of simple, practical, easy ways to demonstrate minimalism and encourage your children to follow you. But even if you have thought of the most enjoyable and amazing plan to do this, practice flexibility too.

If things don't work out, just try again another day. When it comes to dealing with children, sometimes even the best plans don't pan out because children tend to be moody, and if they aren't willing to do something, it can be extremely challenging to convince them. Instead, you should shift your focus to doing something else so you don't end up feeling as frustrated as your little one.

7. Simplify the food they eat

Simplifying your child's food is an excellent way to encourage minimalism. Instead of offering a wide range of options for your child, stick with one or two healthy choices. When your child is still young, you can choose the food for them. But as they grow up, you can encourage them to make choices by presenting options. Just make sure that the options you give them have similar tastes and nutritional value so they don't end up choosing the "unhealthy option" time and time again.

8. Don't place too much importance on toys

Toys are an important part of any child's life, but you shouldn't treat them as such. Yes, children love toys, but these are still material possessions, and you want to avoid placing too much focus on them. Try not to buy too many toys for your children. And for the few toys that you do give, make sure to teach your child how to care for these properly, so they last for a long time. But when it comes to playing, encourage your child to branch out so their world won't revolve around the colorful pieces of plastic or wood that come from stores.

Play with your child and tell the other members of your family to do the same. That way, your child will learn that people and relationships are more important than material things. If they see and understand this early on, this is the kind of thinking they will have even when they grow into teenagers and adults.

As you can see, minimalism can be applied to people of different ages, even to young babies and children. The only difference is that for young individuals, parents have to guide them so they can learn what minimalism is all about. But with a lot of time, patience, and love, even young children can become minimalists and carry the values they learn as they grow into well-rounded adults.

CHAPTER 8:

KIDS AND TEENS ARE THE MINIMALISTS OF TOMORROW

Kids and teenagers often have a difficult time transitioning through the most confusing years of their lives. As a parent, you have already succeeded in overcoming these challenges, and now, you are raising children who are going through the same thing. Kids and teenagers of all ages are faced with change and adversity. Sadly, they often are unaware of what is causing their anxieties and fears. And when you try to find out what is causing all of these negativities, you may discover that chaos is a very common culprit.

Fortunately, minimalism is an excellent ideology for kids and teenagers. When you help them come up with a simple set of rules by which they can live their lives, you are also helping them get rid of unnecessary things, feelings, and emotions. Kids and teens are very vulnerable; therefore, they may need your assistance to face the challenges of life and get through them as unscathed as possible.

While you cannot protect your children from all the changes and challenges that come their way, the best thing you can do is arm them with the skills they need to face these challenges head-on. Since minimalism helps calm the mind while allowing you to focus more on the things that are valuable in life, teaching this concept and all the tips and strategies you have learned can help them cope with life better and in a more positive way. This will bring you closer to your children while helping them learn how to prioritize relationships too. Also, teaching minimalism to kids and teenagers makes them see their family as their main support system that they can rely on no matter what comes their way. Minimalism will not only bring peace to your life. It will also bring your family closer together in ways you didn't even know were possible in the past.

The Modern-Day Challenge of Kids and Teens

Out of all the social categories that exist in the world, the ones who are most focused on living a life of having and wanting are kids and teenagers. In this modern-day world where parents may be too busy trying to earn a living to give their children a "better life," kids and teenagers are left to fend for themselves with a bunch of material things to keep them company. When parents are not around, kids and teens turn to their gadgets which, in turn, bombard them with ads of things they don't need. Aside from these, they also start following influencers and trendsetters who encourage them to want stuff that they don't need because they believe that this stuff will make them happier. But then, after they finally coax their parents into providing them with all of this stuff, they realize that they still feel lonely and empty.

When we reminisce about the "good old days," it makes us feel nostalgic. There is a certain sense of yearning that comes with remembering the simplicity of life in the past. Although I'm not saying that our parents had it easy back then when they were raising us, there are certain issues and challenges we face with kids and teens of this generation that didn't exist in the past. These include:

1. **Entitlement**

    These days, kids and teens feel like they are more entitled to perks and material possessions. And when they don't get these things or situations don't work out as they expected, they

87

immediately feel unhappy. Although there is more stuff to keep kids and teens entertained these days, this also comes with a sense of entitlement that's very difficult to get rid of.

2. Fear of missing out

As kids and teens spend all of their time with their friends both online and offline, they develop a fear of missing out. Browsing through social media profiles and seeing other people living their lives to the fullest makes them feel like their lives aren't exciting, extravagant, or happy enough. Because of this, they expect their parents to give them the same kind of life or else they will miss out on a lot of things. But as a parent, you know that there is no truth to this at all.

3. Anxiety

This is another feeling kids and teens get when they feel like they don't own enough, or they're not good enough. And again, this is mainly caused by the modern-day influences that they are exposed to each day. If your kid or teen feels anxious about their lives, you should help them out. And you can only do this if you spend time with them instead of worrying about all the clutter in your life.

Since minimalism gives you more time to spend with your children, this goes a long way into helping them (and yourself) overcome these challenges. After fully understanding minimalism and applying it to your life gradually, you can start being the influencer in your child's life, and this time, you influence them to embrace a minimalist lifestyle too. Show your kids or teens that minimalism isn't a bad thing. In fact, the more positive you are about it, the more they will see the good effects that come with it too. Then you can try applying these simple and practical tips to encourage your kids and teens to become minimalist members of your family:

1. Invite them to join you

As you start getting rid of the things you don't need, invite your kids or teens to join you. Since you will be starting small, this task won't seem difficult at all. As you sort through your things and declutter, you are also showing them that it's okay to let things go, especially if you don't need them anymore.

2. **Set a schedule for decluttering their things**

After inviting them to help you declutter your own things, set a schedule for them too. Don't force them into this task and start off slow, just like you did at the beginning of your minimalist journey. You can set a decluttering schedule once a week or once a month. In fact, it would be even better if you ask your child to set the schedule, so it doesn't feel like you're imposing this on them. Then once the schedule rolls around, help them declutter the different areas of their lives.

3. **Establish minimalism boundaries**

Boundaries are important for any endeavor. Just because you're the parent, you don't have the right to force your children to get rid of things that matter to them. Before you start decluttering with your kid or teen, help them come up with a set of boundaries. This is an excellent way to teach them the importance of rules while also teaching them to have accountability for their own actions. If they played a part in establishing the rules and boundaries, they are more likely to follow them.

4. **For young kids, make cleanup a simpler task**

It's quite challenging to teach kids how to clean up after playing no matter how few or how many their toys are. Imagine how much time it would take if your child has a huge collection of toys! You can teach decluttering to young children too, but don't get rid of too many things too fast. This might make your child sad, thus, making minimalism a negative thing for them. As you get rid of the toys they don't need little by little, you can teach them how to organize the rest of the toys they own by making things simpler for them. Provide your child with bins, trays, boxes, and other storage containers for them to keep their toys in. Then when they're done playing with their toys or it's time for them to turn in for the night, teach them how to keep their toys in the containers you have provided. This is an excellent way to train your children to become organized early on.

5. **Solve one issue at a time**

Remember the tip about avoiding multitasking? This is more important for kids and teens as they tend to lose focus more easily. When teaching the principles and strategies of minimalism, do so one at a time. In the same way, if your kid or teen is dealing with problems in their lives, help them solve these problems one by one. Taking things step by step makes things more manageable for everyone.

Another important thing to keep in mind when dealing with kids and teens is to take it easy on them. Don't force them to do things repeatedly or continuously as this might exacerbate the negative emotions they have, especially anxiety. Minimalism is a way of life. This means that you don't have to teach it all in one go. It's better to go slow and focus on encouraging them so that minimalism becomes something they want to achieve, not something they want to avoid.

It's Never Too Early or Too Late to Teach Minimalism

Minimalism is an excellent ideology to introduce to kids and teens early on. But even if you have only discovered the wonders of this lifestyle now that you have older teens in your home, you can still introduce this concept. In fact, you might even find it easier to teach minimalism to older teenagers as they can understand abstract concepts better than younger teens and kids. The point is—minimalism can bring a lot of clarity into their chaotic and confusing lives. If you notice that your youngsters don't seem happy with their lives because they don't own things, it's time to change their mindset. Encourage your children to try and do more than what they are doing now. This is one of the most effective ways to answer your kid or teen's questions about why they feel so unhappy. Through minimalism, you can also turn their lives around for the better.

You can teach minimalism to children no matter how young they are. As long as your child can already comprehend things and have conversations with you, they will already have the potential to understand this concept and start following it. But when it comes to minimalism, it should start with you. It won't be very effective if you try to teach your children to become minimalists when you don't practice the same strategies. After showing off your minimalist skills to your kids and teens, give these other tips a try:

1. **Have a conversation about minimalism**

   For your children to understand what minimalism means, you must have a conversation about it. Tailor your conversation to your child's age and levels of comprehension. For instance, if you have a 6-year-old, you should explain minimalism as learning how to let go of things that are unnecessary or the things that are bringing you down. Most kids won't understand this. Instead, you can tell your child that they have too many things and all these things can't fit in your home. You need to get rid of some things so that you have space to move around. And you can give those things away to other little boys and girls who don't have toys to play with.

   This is just a simple example of how you can explain minimalism to a young child. If you need to, incorporate stories and songs to your explanation. The key here is to try to make your child understand this abstract concept in the simplest way possible.

2. **Allow them to grow and change at their own pace**

   After explaining the concept of minimalism and giving your

kids and teens some tips on how to practice it, don't force their progress. Kids and teens develop at their own pace and this is something that you have to understand. Be patient with them and fill their lives with encouragement through every step. This makes things better for them and it also brings you closer together as a family.

3. **Guide them throughout the process**

    After teaching minimalism in different ways, you need to step back and simply be there to guide them throughout the process. If your kid or teen makes a mistake, don't scold them for it. Instead, use this as a learning opportunity for them to understand what minimalism is. And if your kid or teen shows progress, celebrate it no matter how small. For instance, if your child runs up to you and announces that they found something they want to give away without you asking for it, show appreciation for this gesture. Even if it is just one small thing, treat it as something big.

Remember that positivity works better than anything else. Also, remember that you want to grow closer as a family. The best way to do this is by incorporating positivity into the different aspects of your minimalist journey, especially when it comes to teaching minimalism to your kids and teens.

Minimalism for Teens

Minimalism for children is a simple thing because you can only give them simple explanations and tips. But if you are raising teens, things can get a bit more complicated. Generally, if you want your teen to get better, you can share with them some simple minimalist rules that will also help them live a better life. But before you can do this, you must understand a few things about minimalism for teens:

- Each day, our world grows more and more materialistic.

- Influencers, trendsetters, and advertisers are intentionally targeting teens as they are very impressionable.
- Teens place a high value on conformity and acceptance with their peers.
- Teens are still in the process of exploring their ability to make decisions. Because of this, they might not place a high value on input coming from you.
- Since they are still young, most of the significant decisions in their lives are still ahead of them. When they understand minimalism, they will also have the capacity to make wiser decisions.
- The spending habits of teens aren't fully formed yet. At this stage, these habits are being shaped, and you can play a role in helping them build positive habits in terms of spending.
- Teens aren't in debt—yet. Because of this, they don't know how it feels to be in debt, thus, they tend to be more lax when it comes to spending. This is another area where you must provide guidance.

Yes, there will be challenges when you start teaching your teen minimalism. But as long as you motivate your teen and provide the guidance they need, they may be able to start their own minimalism journey along with you. Here are some things you can do to help move the process along:

- **Model simplicity while encouraging idealism**

  Even with teens, it's more effective to show what needs to be done than to just talk about it. While you may explain what minimalism is and how your teen can become a minimalist, showing them *how* it's done is better. And as you show them the benefits of simple living by modeling how to achieve it, keep the encouragement coming. That way, they don't lose their idealism as they try to adopt a new lifestyle that they aren't used to.

93

- **Help them accept—and deal—with adversity and change**

  The teenage years are a very confusing time in a person's life. Throughout these years, your teen will experience ups, downs, and a lot of uncertainty. As you take the journey of minimalism with them, guide them through these difficult times too. You don't have to coddle your teen or fight their battles. Just be there when they need you.

  You can even apply this to the strategies of minimalism. For instance, when it's time for you to help your teen declutter, this is definitely a huge change that they must deal with. Guide them through the process, and again, don't force them into it. Since teens are older than kids, you can explain how this change will benefit their lives and the lives of everyone else in your family. Helping your teen deal with adversity and change in a positive way makes them stronger and more resilient individuals.

- **Discourage entitlement**

  Since entitlement is one of the biggest challenges you will face as a parent, then you should discourage this as much as possible. Fortunately, there are many ways you can do this. For one, you can teach your children how to budget and save money. And when they want to buy something expensive, have them pay for it themselves.

  Also, try to explain to your teen that there are things in life that they cannot and will not be able to control. Share examples from your own life to help them understand this better. This is one lesson that helps them let go of things more easily like material possessions, negative emotions, and so on. The key here is to help your teen realize that they don't always deserve the things that they want. Often, they have to work to get what they want, and this is much more satisfying in the end.

- **Encourage them to let go**

  Most teens are very personal and protective when it comes to the things that they own. Because of this, letting go might not be as easy for them as it is for you or for younger children. This is where conversations come into play. You can share with your teen the benefits minimalism has brought to your life and how it can potentially improve their lives as well. In fact, you can even share everything you have learned and will learn in this book to help them understand things better. Once your teen understands the power of minimalism, they will show more willingness to declutter with you.

- **Start decluttering**

  At this point, your teen should already understand that material things aren't the most important thing in the world. Intangible things like their identity, their relationships, and others are immensely more important in life as these are the things that will make them authentically happy. So now, you can start decluttering with your teen. Here are some steps to guide you:

  o For this task, you need to prepare two containers—one for things to donate and another for things to throw away. For the things your teen wants to keep, you can either place them in a third container or rearrange those items in your teen's room.

  o Choose one area of the room to focus on each time you have a decluttering session. It would take too much time to declutter an entire room. This task might also be too overwhelming. Therefore, you should work on one area at a time and set a regular schedule for this task.

  o As you work, ask your teen challenging questions to help them determine whether they should donate, throw away or keep the items in their room. Continue doing this until you have successfully decluttered the whole room.

If you notice your teen struggling with the task, take a break. Talk about how they feel and when they are overwhelmed, help them through it. Don't be too strict with your teen. Encourage them and help them see the value of what you are trying to achieve. Only then can you convince your teen to start becoming a true minimalist.

CHAPTER 9:

GIVING UP SHOULD NEVER BE AN OPTION

By now, you should have a more positive perspective of minimalism. After all, it's not just about living with as few material possessions as possible. Rather, it is more about being intentional in your life and finding ways to let go of everything you don't need—not just your possessions. Through minimalism, you can value and appreciate the things that really matter, thus, making you a happier member of your family.

Minimalism is a journey. It isn't something you decide to do and adopt in a day. However, when you face challenges along the way, giving up should never be an option. As with any other change in life, minimalism will take time, effort, patience, and love. As long as you have these, becoming a minimalist is much easier. To help inspire you to keep going, here are some dos and don'ts for you to ponder on:

As a minimalist, DO:

- Know your reason for wanting to become a minimalist. This will also serve as your motivation to keep moving forward even if you encounter challenges.
- Make plans for how you will apply minimalism throughout your life. You have already learned a lot of tips in this book,

but we're not done yet! By the end, you would have all you need to create a plan for how your minimalist journey will commence.

- Be as realistic as possible throughout your journey. Don't be too hard on yourself or your family so you don't lose your drive to keep going. Decluttering and other aspects of becoming a minimalist require self-kindness. The more you practice this, the easier it becomes for you to apply the strategies of minimalism for yourself and the rest of your family.

- Practice gratitude and appreciation. When you have these, you will realize that living a life with less is actually a blessing. You will have more time to share with your family, thus, allowing you to deal with any issues that have been plaguing your relationships.

- Take your time. Just as Rome wasn't built in a day, minimalism doesn't happen overnight. The good things will come as long as you keep practicing minimalism while keeping your purpose in mind.

As a minimalist, DON'T:

- Compare your life with the lives of everyone else. Remember that you are trying to become a minimalist to change your life for the better. But if you keep getting caught up in what everyone else is doing, you will end up getting stuck in the same situation you are currently in.

- Focus only on material possessions. Minimalism is about decluttering your life from everything unnecessary and everything that weighs you down. It's not just about getting rid of stuff.

- Use decluttering as an excuse for you to purchase more. The more you declutter your home, the emptier it may look. Therefore, you might want to replace all of the things you've let go of with newer and shinier things. Again, if you do this, you might find yourself unable to move forward because your stuff just keeps piling up.

Also, don't expect that minimalism will solve all of your problems. This lifestyle can pave the way for you to deal with your problems in better ways. Through minimalism, you can focus more on your family instead of material things and other unnecessary aspects of your life. When this happens, things may start falling into place for you.

Building New Habits

To become a true minimalist, you should learn how to break your old habits—such as spending too much, collecting too many things, distracting yourself with everything but your relationships—and replace these with new habits that fit into the minimalist lifestyle better. Building new habits takes a lot of effort and time. Just like minimalism, this doesn't happen overnight. But the good news is, when it comes to minimalism, the habits you must build aren't complicated or difficult at all. And the more you practice them, the more they will become part of your life. The trick is to just keep at it and never, ever give up. Here are some tips for you:

1. **Make small changes**

   When you make small changes to your life, this makes things easier and more manageable for you. For instance, instead of attempting to declutter your entire home in a month, create a schedule for decluttering the different areas in your home one at a time. Another example is when you go shopping. Instead of restricting yourself from buying anything, give yourself some choices. For instance, if you're used to buying all flavors of snacks for your family, minimize this by only buying the most popular flavor among the members of your family.

   It's a lot easier to stick with small changes in your lifestyle than big ones that cause a lot of chaos and confusion. Once you get used to those small changes, you can start making even more changes over time. Soon, you won't even realize that you have

99

already made a lot of changes in your life and these changes have already become your habits.

2. Focus on the things that you have

Instead of focusing on what is missing in your life, focus on everything that you have right now. This makes it easier for you to let things go and apply the other tips and strategies you have learned thus far. Consciously focusing on the good things in your life will naturally make you more grateful and appreciative. And once you move on to strengthening your relationships with your family members, you will realize that they also belong to the category of things (and people) that you have and that you should be thankful for.

3. Clear surfaces regularly

This is one simple habit that you can practice to make decluttering easier. The thing about minimalism is that it's an ongoing process. You cannot just declutter your home then go back to your old ways. Whenever you see an empty surface in your home, you place something new on it. Soon, you'll see that your home has been invaded by unnecessary material possessions once again. Instead, practice the habit of clearing your home's surfaces regularly. Whenever you see things on surfaces that don't belong there, remove them. Find where those items belong or if you don't have to keep them, throw those items away.

4. Learn how to be more organized

Just like decluttering, organization is an integral part of minimalism. Since you will be coming up with a plan of how you will become a minimalist, you should also learn how to be more organized along the way. Organizing your life makes it simpler which, in essence, is what minimalism is all about. Fortunately, there are many habits you can build to become more organized, like creating to-do lists, planning your meals, creating a schedule for decluttering your home, and more. Despite this, though, you should still be flexible enough to accept the unexpected and just roll with it so you don't get stressed.

5. **Detach your self-worth from your material possessions**

    This is another habit that you should consciously work on as you become a minimalist. In the past, you may have always associated your self-worth with your material possessions. For instance, being able to buy the newest gadgets as soon as they come out makes you cooler. Or owning a big house packed with material possessions makes you more accomplished. It's time to eliminate this way of thinking. Instead, focus on the good things that make you who you are. These are more valuable in determining your self-worth than anything that money can buy.

Finally, you should also build the habit of encouraging and motivating yourself. If you don't want to give up on your minimalist journey, you must know exactly how to motivate yourself to keep going. You should know what drives you and inspires you the most. And you should use these things to help you achieve success in terms of your minimalist goals.

Understanding the Minimalist Way of Living

Apart from motivating yourself so you don't give up on this endeavor, understanding the minimalist way of living allows you to make this a permanent part of your life. To do this, keep these things in mind:

1. **Minimalism isn't just a passing trend... it's a way of living**

    These days, there are so many trends and fads that only last for a short while before fading away. Minimalism shouldn't be one of these. If you really want to live a minimalist life, you should work on it. Keep practicing the tips you have learned, keep building new habits that promote minimalism, and keep encouraging your family to do the same. This is the best way for you to make minimalism your lifestyle instead of a passing trend.

2. Respect the decisions of your family members no matter what these are

Even if you can explain what minimalism is to your family, this doesn't mean that they will get on board right away. Respect this decision of theirs. Don't force them to become minimalists as this might make things worse than they already are. If some members of your family adopt minimalism because of your influence, appreciate them for it. If not, continue to show them love, support, and your real self. This lets your family know that you accept them for who they are, for what decisions they make, and for how they choose to live their lives. Eventually, they might join you and the rest of your minimalist family. Then you can share this wonderful lifestyle with everyone who matters most in your life.

3. Continue decluttering regularly

It's important to continue decluttering your home and your life even after you have gone through your entire home. Clutter has a way of creeping back into your life. To prevent this from happening, make decluttering a regular part of your life. Keep doing it until it becomes a habit that contributes to your minimalist lifestyle.

4. Use your time wisely

The longer you practice minimalism, the simpler your life becomes. And the simpler your life becomes, the more you will have free time to do other things. As a minimalist, make sure that you always fill your spare time with important things. Don't waste your time staring at your phone while playing games or browsing through social media. Instead, use this time to connect with the members of your family. Get to know them more, spend quality time with them, and continue reaching out to solidify your connections and make your family happy, whole, and content with your lives.

5. **Make sure that everything is always in its place**

Just as you would declutter things regularly, make sure that everything in your home is in its place. This helps you stay focused on the important things, as well as on your minimalist journey. If you can keep things simple and orderly at home, minimalism comes more naturally to you.

Minimalism starts in the mind. But when you express it through your actions, you will learn how to live your life as a minimalist. You won't have to worry about material, emotional, mental, and physical clutter anymore. Understanding minimalism and applying it to your life is the key that will unlock the door to the new life you want to have with your family.

CHAPTER 10:

DIGITAL MINIMALISM FOR IMPROVED MENTAL HEALTH

This last chapter is very important as digital minimalism is one of the newer things we have to deal with. In the past, people didn't have to worry about technology taking over their lives in the same way it does now. We are now living in the digital age, but, sadly, technology often takes a toll on family relationships, especially when not used correctly. Fortunately, practicing digital minimalism can help preserve your mental health, as well as your relationships with your family.

When you walk into a restaurant, do you hear a lot of chatter or is it more common to see people in tables immersed in the digital world as they stare at their phones while waiting for their food? Often, the latter is the case. In particular, social media has become such a huge part of our lives and it's starting to make us mentally sick. We may not notice this and we may not even accept it, but the truth is, so many of us have become addicted to social media that we have forgotten how to live and interact with others in the real world.

As a minimalist, you should try to eliminate this addiction from your life and the lives of the rest of your family. After all, it will be very difficult to try spending quality time with your family when all they want to do is play games, listen to music, watch videos, and browse through their social media profiles all day long. Unless you can help them minimize their addiction to these devices that open the doors to the digital world, you cannot truly live life as a minimalist family. Don't worry though, because this is entirely possible. This is another process you have to go through on the path to minimalism and it might just be the most challenging one.

The Dangers of the Digital World

While the digital world may seem more comfortable, it isn't great for your mental health. Social media, the Internet, and the rest of the digital world have a considerable impact on your mental health that is usually negative, and it tends to spread like wildfire. Because of this, millions and millions of people in this digital age are now struggling with mental health issues because they focus too much on technology.

The explosion of the digital world's popularity came out of nowhere. Once we were introduced to the Internet, things snowballed out of control, and now, we find ourselves living in a world where our online lives have become much more important than our real lives. This is one of the saddest realities of life now, and yet, most people refuse to acknowledge it.

I have to admit that in my own minimalist journey, practicing digital minimalism was one of the most challenging things I had to do—and it wasn't fun for the rest of my family either. As I reflected on how much I relied on technology and how much I was invested in the digital world, I realized that just like everyone else, I was in too deep. I loved watching television, I enjoyed playing games on my tablet, and I always felt the need to keep checking my phone to see if I had new emails, notifications, messages, and more. But the minute I consciously put my devices away and started focusing on my family, things changed for the better.

The most significant danger of the digital world is that it initiates a kind of devolution. Instead of evolving and improving our emotional, relational, and intellectual abilities, technology tends to have the opposite effect. Each day, after you spend time in the digital world, your ability to self-reflect and contemplate weakens. Instead, your mind is filled with unnecessary information, and worse, you are left with nothing else to think about but how seemingly perfect the lives of other people are. Because of this, you try to compete with them by pushing yourself harder at work so that you can have the same luxurious lives as those you see on social media.

The more time you spend in the digital world, the more your social skills start deteriorating as you lose your ability to empathize, listen, and interact with others. Instead, you just keep thinking about other people's lives and how you wish you could be as happy as them. But in reality, these profiles and photographs are merely facades for people who are trying to let other people believe that they are living perfect lives.

Don't let this happen to you!

It's time to save yourself and your family from this unrealistic world. It's time for you to start focusing on each other to strengthen your bonds and the love you have for each other. And the best way to do this is through digital minimalism—the most modern aspect of the minimalist lifestyle.

Applying Minimalism the Right Way

When you apply digital minimalism to your life, you can use it to declutter your mind so you won't be too focused on your digital world. The fact is, when you spend too much time in the digital world, everything that happens in it starts affecting how you think and, eventually, who you are. We cannot control what happens in the digital world. All we get to do is stand by, contribute when we want to, and watch as other people brag about how great their lives are, even though their reality is far from what they share. Over time, you start feeling discontent about who you are, about the things you own, and even about your family. There's no time like the present to start minimizing your digital world and here are a few simple yet effective tips to start you off:

106

1. **Set time limits for your gadget and social media usage**

    During your digital detox, there's no need to get rid of your gadgets right away. After all, minimalism isn't about going extreme. Instead, you might want to create a schedule for your gadget and social media usage so you can shorten the time you spend with and on them. For instance, while enjoying a break at work, you can give yourself time to browse through your social media profiles. But as soon as your break ends, so should the time you spend browsing, liking, sharing, and so on. Or you can set time limits for yourself during the weekends to play games on your gadgets. As long as they don't interfere with your work, your decluttering efforts and other minimalist strategies, and, of course, your time with your family, gadget and social media usage don't have to be a bad thing.

2. **Turn off your notifications**

    Probably the most time-consuming and distracting things from the digital world are notifications. You have email notifications, Facebook notifications, game notifications, and so much more. And as soon as you hear that familiar sound that indicates notifications, you get distracted from whatever you are doing. Then you pick up your phone and get lost in the digital world once again. To avoid this from happening, go through your phone's settings and turn off any notifications that can wait. That way, you only get notified when something really important comes. When you have free time, that is when you can go through your other notifications.

3. **Turn off your phone at night**

    As a minimalist, it's not recommended to turn in when your phone is turned on. No matter how much you fight it, you will be tempted to pick up your phone, especially when you cannot sleep. But if you use your phone as an alarm clock or you don't want to miss any messages, the best thing you can do is set it to silent mode so it doesn't distract you throughout the night.

4. **Find out what truly matters in your digital world... and get rid of the rest**

   Just because the digital world can have a negative impact on your life, this doesn't mean that everything about it is bad. Over time, there are things in the digital world that have become meaningful to you. As a minimalist, you should identify what these things are so you can keep them and gradually get rid of the rest. For instance, if you can only connect with family members or relatives in another country through one of the apps on your phone, keep that app. But if you have a gaming app or a social media app that does nothing but take up your time, you may want to get rid of it. Just as you would declutter in the real world, decluttering in your digital world will go a long way for your own benefit and for the benefit of your family.

5. **Reconnect with the real world**

   After disconnecting yourself from the real world, the next thing to do is reconnect with the real world. You can do this by reaching out to friends, relatives, and family members who don't live in your home. Also, spend more time with the members of your family. Rediscover the things you love about them and introduce fun things for them to do. While this won't happen overnight, reconnecting with the real world is one of the most fulfilling things you can ever do for yourself.

As you can see, all of these strategies are simple, practical, and effective. And the best part is, once you have mastered them, you can start encouraging your spouse and children to do the same thing.

CONCLUSION:

TRANSFORMING YOUR FAMILY AND YOUR HOME THROUGH MINIMALISM

There you have it—everything you need to know about minimalism to transform yourself, your home, and your family through a life of living with less. As you will soon discover, minimalism will change your life in wonderful ways. Personally, I had a lot of fun writing this book and I hope you had just as much fun and enlightenment reading it. Although everything you may have learned about minimalism here is mainly based on my experiences and the experiences of my family, once you apply the tips, strategies, and the actual concept of minimalism to your life, you will have your own priceless experiences with your family along the way.

From start to finish, I have shared with you countless information, tips, and strategies to help you start your minimalist journey. We started off by defining minimalism and a short history of this fantastic lifestyle. Then we focused on family to help you become aware of the most common issues you may encounter along with how to solve these issues and some tips on how to transform your family's life through minimalism. Next, we learned about the home—the place where you and your family should build stronger connections and relationships with each other. Creating a minimalist home by working together as a family is both enjoyable and fulfilling.

After introducing minimalism to your family and transforming your home into one where a minimalist family resides, it's time to start working on your relationships with your family. The next chapter discussed the importance of family relationships and how you can strengthen them through minimalism. Then we moved on to learning about the power of doing versus having. As a minimalist, you shouldn't focus on having too many material possessions and other unnecessary things in your life. Instead, you should focus on doing things to improve your family life and bring you closer together.

Then we dug into decluttering—one of the most important aspects of minimalism. Decluttering your life can happen in many ways. Fortunately, you have already learned the most practical and effective ways in this chapter. The next two chapters focused on the members of the family—the parents and the children of varying ages. As a parent, you can apply minimalism to your life to make your parenting journey smoother and more effective. Then we discussed the different ways you can help your children adopt minimalism too, whether they are toddlers, young children, or teens.

Chapter 9 contained the most inspiring message of this book which is to never give up. Minimalism doesn't happen overnight. You have to constantly work on becoming a minimalist until it has transformed all the aspects of your life for the better. Here, you learned how to build new habits while understanding minimalism to the fullest. The final chapter was a bonus chapter as it delved into the modern-day issue of digital clutter. This is something we must also deal with, especially when it comes to teaching minimalism to your children in this digital, fast-paced world.

As you can see, this book contained a wide range of topics to help you understand minimalism in the most profound way possible. As promised at the beginning of the book, I have shared with you the best solution to simplify your life to make you happier, more fulfilled, and more stress-free. If there is one thing I would like you to take away from this book, that is to start your own journey as soon as possible.

Don't let time pass you by. Through minimalism, you can focus on the things that truly matter. And when your whole family lives this way, you can declutter your lives together and come out happier, healthier, and stronger than ever.

I'd Love Your Help

As a self-publishing author, reviews are the lifeblood of my work.

I would be over-the-moon thankful if you could take just 60 seconds to leave a brief review on Amazon.

I know you must be busy and I truly appreciate your time, even a few short sentences would be greatly helpful.

Don't forget to get your complimentary

ACTIVITIES FOR A MINIMALIST FAMILY

Fun Activities to Declutter Your Home and Heart

How awesome that you've come this far! I hope you've enjoyed the book and begin your minimalism journey as a family.

What's in store with this particular download:

- The complete list of minimalism activities for your family;
- Practical ways to enjoy these activities at home;
- Advice on how to go beyond the activities and become a true minimalist.

Minimalism is a great choice for you and your family regardless of your past experiences.

Click the link below to get your free activities ideas:

http://gracestockholm.net/activities-of-a-minimalist-family

BONUS SECTION:
GUIDED MEDITATION FOR PARENTS AND KIDS

In this bonus section, I have prepared 2 special guided meditation sessions.

The first is for you, the parent. The second session is for your child. Both are designed to help you and your child absorb and become comfortable with all aspects of minimalism. The practice is suitable for children of all ages. Depending on your child's age, you may want to sit with your child for this session, at least for the first few times. If you have a younger child and the session is too long for them, simply do a few minutes at a time and gradually increase the meditation time.

If this is the audio version, just dive in.

If this is the kindle or paperback version, sit down and read it to yourself slowly.

Session #1 - For You

-Welcome to this meditation practice. In this session, we will be focusing on the most important things we can while meditating, decluttering the mind from all of its everyday chaos, chatter, and talks. We will calm our minds not by taking part in the chaos, but by taking a step back, listening, and understanding the mind. And then letting go.

-The idea of decluttering is best known from minimalism. We will now start to explore the different stages of the mind and how they will help us declutter from unwanted thoughts and emotions. Let's get ready to sit back and enjoy this hour of stillness and relaxation.

-Begin by finding a spot where you can comfortably sit for the next hour or so. It can be a chair, the bed, the couch in your living room, or simply the floor. Wherever you want, simply sit down and find that comfortable posture, one you can hold for an extended period without the body becoming tense.

-Once you're all set in, it is now the time to focus on your breathing for the first couple of moments of the practice. Simply notice the breath going in and then going out of your chest. As the body breathes, it creates the natural rising and falling sensation of the chest. Place your hands in the middle of your torso and feel where the breath is getting formed right now.

-You don't have to change anything about it, simply notice where the breath forms and how it moves towards the body. Is the breath forming in the abdomen? Is the breath manifesting in the chest area? Or is the breath appearing somewhere in between the two?

-If you've found the point of your breath, you can now move the hand back to a comfortable position, be it in your lap or simply beside you if you're lying flat on the floor. And as you do so, notice the breath one more time as it moves naturally throughout your body.

-Now take a couple of big, deep breaths in through the nose and then out through the mouth. You don't have to do any thinking right now. Your mind can be free from thought as you focus solely on the powerful breaths that you're taking. Nothing else is important at this moment. Breathing heavier than normal helps you get a better grasp of where you are right now, how you are feeling, and what is actually happening in the body.

-Simply breathe like this for a few moments, deeply in through the nose, and then out through the mouth. Take your time and make the breaths long, but comfortable at the same time. As you're breathing in and out, remember to focus on the idea of the breath giving your body the fuel it needs to be alive.

-And with this last exhale, gently closing the eyes and letting the breath come back to its natural state, in and out through the nose.

-Before diving into the decluttering of the mind, we're going to start the practice by scanning the body. We will begin with the top part, the head and neck, and then move all the way down to the feet. While we go down the body, we will perform a decluttering of all the tension and stress that we've gathered throughout the day today. We will notice them and then, without any judgment, let them go before moving to the next part of the body.

-Begin with the top of your head. Scan the very top of your head to see if it is in any way tense or stressed. Notice the physical sensations that you can feel. If there are no sensations, that's completely fine. If there's any tension, it is now a good thing to let it go without judging or overthinking it too much.

-All of the tension at the top of the head is now gone.

-Moving on downwards, scan the entirety of the head. See if the face, the back of the head, or even the neck have some tensed areas. If they do, again, it is no good if you judge them. Judging a pain or a tensed muscle will only make them more painful. Noticing them and not interfering with them will make the stress disappear in an effortless manner.

-Great, all of the stress in your head, face, back of the head and neck is now gone.

-You can now notice the way the chest and the upper back feel. Scanning the body is the best way to come back into the self and notice how you truly feel. Is there any tension or unease in the chest area? Is the heart beating regularly, or is it beating a little faster or slower than usual? Is the upper back relaxed, or is there any pain or discomfort somewhere in there? Regardless of the answer, all you have to do is to notice the feeling, and then let go of it.

-Perfect, there is no more tension in the chest and upper back now.

-It is now time to scan the lower back area and the abdomen, the stomach, and all other crucial internal organs of the body. The machinery that makes you who you are is not just in the heart or brain.

116

Every single organ in your body is responsible for keeping you alive. Even the smallest, most hidden one can make or break you. Is there any tension in this part of the body? Notice the stress points, and then let the stress go.

-There is no more tension in the lower back, abdomen, and stomach from now on.

-You have now reached the top part of your legs and can scan right through to the knees. See if there's any pain or discomfort here. If there is, that's fine, simply notice it. If there's no tension, again, no need to change anything here.

-Awesome, your upper legs and knees are now tension-free.

-Finally, you've reached the bottom part of your legs and can now scan all the way to the toes. Have a closer look here and see if there's anything that is bothering you about the way the feet feel right at this moment. If there's a sense of unease, take it into account but do not categorize it as being a bad thing. Simply see it for what it is. This is the only way to let go of the clutter of feelings and sensations the body accumulates over a period of time. Once you mingle with the feelings, you're only giving them space to grow. Noticing them and not doing anything about them will make them naturally vanish away.

-Perfect, you are now without tension in the lower legs and feet.

-Before moving further with today's practice, I want you to take a moment to really appreciate the way you feel right at this moment. The way the body is free from all tension, from all stress, from all pain and unease. Take a second to make a mental picture of the way the body is right now. And keep this mental image of the tensionless body with you throughout the day.

-After the body, it is now time to declutter the mind. It is now time to get rid of all thoughts, all emotions and feelings that derive from those thoughts. Just as minimalism teaches us how important it is to live with less, to have a home that's free from stuff we don't need, so it says about the mind and how crucial it is for it to be free from worry,

117

anxiety and negative thinking.

-The problem is people think you can control the mind and force it to become the way you want it to become. If you try to make the mind calm, the mind will do exactly the opposite and become restless. If you want the mind to be relaxed and not think, the next thing it does is to think about everything and all at the same time.

-The only way to declutter the mind is to not intervene in the thinking process. Once you accept the thoughts that arise in the mind the way they come to you, you are creating a certain space in the mind that will turn into a place for the thoughts to go through. When you create the space between you and your thoughts, the thoughts will naturally go away without affecting you.

-Never believe your thoughts to be you. If you don't identify with the thoughts that pop up in your mind, there's never going to be a clutter of them anywhere. Let's try this right now.

-Notice any particular thought that comes to mind right now. Focus on the breathing as you do so and as you've been doing for the entirety of the practice. All you have to do is to follow the thought. See where it is going. Is it getting longer, shorter, weaker, stronger? Is it forming into a serious deal with which you're not comfortable to discuss?

-Next, see if the thought is turning into an emotion. Does it make you feel tense, uneasy, restless or emotional in any way? Maybe it makes you feel ecstatic, happy, pleasant? Simply notice the way the emotion is forming from the thought.

-Finally, see if there's a feeling that comes out of the thought. Notice the feeling it creates and then do absolutely nothing else but take it the way it comes.

-By doing so with even a single thought once every other hour or so, you're starting to create a sense of space in your mind. By simply stopping to dispute every thought and emotion or feeling it creates, and just letting it manifest itself, you are free from the sachels of thought cluttering in the mind. The clutter that stops you from thinking straight. And all it takes is for you to stop yourself from mingling with the thoughts.

-See if you can spot another thought that arises in the mind right now. What is the first natural reaction of the mind when that thought comes in? The mind wants to dispute it. It wants to analyze it, to change it, to do something about it. Anything. Training the mind just to observe the thought and not filter it as a good or bad thought is the most important step towards a decluttered, calm, easy, and tension-free mind.

-Have a few moments to yourself now to try and catch a few more thoughts and notice them move around, creating their emotions and feelings, and then letting them go without spending even a drop of your energy on them.

<<PAUSE for a minute to let the meditator focus on letting go of thoughts>>

-All the way until tonight, try to exercise this process of noticing and letting go of the thoughts in the mind. As soon as the thought arises and the mind starts putting up with it, simply say the word "thought" in your mind and let the thought go. Do this for as many times as you can, try to catch as many thoughts as they form and release them before they're turning into feelings or emotions. Keep practicing this all throughout the day today.

-Now that the body and the mind are both cleared and decluttered, we can move along to the final part of the practice. This part is based on the idea of listening to a series of affirmations that can now better be incorporated into your system.

-Just like you'd plant a flower in the cleaned soil, so will we plant these ideas that are transforming into your mind, deep within you. Whenever you need to declutter the mind and the spirit, all you'll have to do is to come back to these ideas and you'll be once again on track.

-Minimalism is all about taking things slow and getting rid of the unnecessary stuff. This is precisely what we will be doing with these affirmations now. Simple, concise phrases that will forever be there for you once they've reached their designated place in the mind. You can access them remotely, without having to go through the meditation again.

-READ THE AFFIRMATIONS SLOWLY, WITH CALM IN YOUR VOICE, GENTLY-

-Let's begin with the very first affirmation of the series. Gently focus your attention on the breath. You're breathing slow and steady, effortless. Here we go, so pay attention.

-**"You succeed in life when all you really want is only what you really need."** Ok, one more time for good measure. **"You have succeeded in life when all you really want is only what you really need."**

-PAUSE FOR 10 SECONDS-

-We, humans, have made it a habit to measure success based on how much or how little we have in the material part of life. We need bigger houses, bigger cars, lots of food and other things. In reality, there's never going to be enough of those to really make us happy. The happiness will come once we learn to feel successful with exactly as much as we have.

-Now, we'll move along to the second affirmation of the day. Let's just focus on these valuable words, as we keep a gentle eye on that breathing and let it all sink in in harmony.

-**"Too many people spend money they haven't earned, to buy things they don't want, to impress people they don't like."** This one is a bit harsh but extremely true. Once more. **"Too many people spend money they haven't earned, to buy things they don't want, to impress people they don't like."**

-PAUSE FOR 10 SECONDS-

-When people think about wealth, they ultimately think about money. But oftentimes people spend money on things they never actually need. You don't need that luxury car. Any car that has four wheels works as well. You don't need that ridiculously expensive handbag. Any handbag that can carry what you need with you should suffice. Trying to impress people is unhealthy. Minimalism is buying only the true necessities, enjoying what we have, and living with the idea of financial freedom in mind.

-All right, let's move to affirmation number three of our series today. Remember to breathe and enjoy the decluttered mind and body that we've achieved so far while listening.

-**"Simplicity is the ultimate sophistication."** This one is by Da Vinci, so let's enjoy the incredible, simple truth again. **"Simplicity is the ultimate sophistication."**

-PAUSE FOR 10 SECONDS-

-As Da Vinci says, it is important to remember that the best things in life are simple. Love is simple. You can either feel it or not. A good meal is often simple. Sleep, the simplest of all things, is so vital and so enhancing for all. One night with no sleep, and you can feel the drawbacks of it entirely. Simplicity is the utmost sophisticated of things. And it often costs close to nothing.

-Well done so far. We'll now be listening to the fourth affirmation of the day. Once again, gently bring the attention back to the breath as you listen to the following words.

-**"The idea of owning, more than anything else, prevents us from living freely and nobly."** Once more, let's listen in. **"The idea of owning, more than anything else, prevents us from living freely and nobly."**

-PAUSE FOR 10 SECONDS-

-Possessions are at the core of our misery. The more you have, the more you'll want to have. It's an endless circle of working more, doing more, but actually feeling less and less. The more you have, the less you can enjoy what you have. The entire idea of owning, of possessing more and more, is what is ultimately stripping us from enjoying the life

121

that we're given, freely and nobly.

Ok, here's the fifth affirmation of the day. Listen in carefully for this one as well. After this one, we'll take a small break in the middle of this part to regroup our mind, breath, and body.

-**"As you simplify your life, the laws of the universe will be simpler; solitude will not be solitude, poverty will not be poverty, nor weakness."** Again. **"As you simplify your life, the laws of the universe will be simpler; solitude will not be solitude, poverty will not be poverty, nor weakness."**

-PAUSE FOR 10 SECONDS-

-A simple life is always going to be a rewarding life. Having less means owning more valuable things rather than a clutter of items that have no meaning to you. A watch your father has gifted you when their time has come will be infinitely more valuable than any luxury watch you can buy at the store. Solitude becomes a strength, not a weakness, when you understand this idea.

-We're in the middle of the affirmations practice today. Let's take a moment to deal with any possible aches in the body, as we're closing in on this meditation, and the body has now rested in the same position for a long time. Stretch your legs and arms, bend your neck, relax your back but keep the overall posture the same.

-Focus on the breath now, regroup your breathing. If it was getting out of its gentle rhythm, now it's the time to regain that soft control, becoming aware of it completely. Breathe in through the nose and then out through the mouth. Continue to do so, as we move along with the following affirmations now.

-All right, let's listen to affirmation number six. As with the previous ones, we'll be focusing on each and every word, while gently keeping focus on the breathing that we do consciously.

-**"Reduce the complexity of life by eliminating the needless wants of life, and the labors of life reduce themselves."** Nice, once more, listen in. **"Reduce the complexity of life by eliminating the needless wants of life, and the labors of life reduce themselves."**

-PAUSE FOR 10 SECONDS-

-When talking about minimalism, it's important to notice that this is not applying just for decluttering your house of all the stuff you don't need. This also applies to urges and things that you want and are not material. Controlling sudden urges to do this and that, although they're entirely avoidable, is also important. The more you reduce the complexity of your life, the better.

-We've arrived at the seventh affirmation of the day now. Let's listen in and focus on what this one has in store for us. Keep a gentle focus on the breath as you listen along.

-**"The secret of happiness is not found in seeking more, but in developing the capacity to enjoy less."** One more time. **"The secret of happiness is not found in seeking more, but in developing the capacity to enjoy less."**

-PAUSE FOR 10 SECONDS-

-Happiness is so abstract. It means something else for basically each and every single one of us. For me, it can be reading a good book in front of the fire. For you, it can be spending time with your pet. For most of us, though, happiness has become so complex, it's hard to even think about it. When in reality, happiness is enjoying the things you have. Less happiness is more happiness.

-Affirmation number eight is next. Let's go ahead and listen to this one now. Follow the breath as you follow each word.

-**"The ability to simplify means to eliminate the unnecessary so that the necessary may speak."** And one more time now. **"The ability to simplify means to eliminate the unnecessary so that the necessary may speak."**

-PAUSE FOR 10 SECONDS-

-When dealing with a situation, it is crucial to distinguish between what's important and what's background noise. When you can instinctively see what is needed, and able to leave anything else behind, the necessary part of your existence will naturally begin to speak. Guiding you towards a better tomorrow, helping you instead of staying in your path.

-This is our ninth affirmation coming up right now, so let's go ahead and see how this one sounds like. Remember to breathe calmly, focusing on the lessons in this next part.

-**"The simplest things are often the truest."** Again. **"The simplest things are often the truest."**

-PAUSE FOR 10 SECONDS-

-Truth is so simple. It's ridiculously so sometimes. They say no matter how big a truth is, or how small it is, a truth is a truth even if only one person believes it. Simple things are almost entirely true. The blooming of a flower. The birth of a child. The awakening of nature in the spring. These are universal truths that can't be changed. Truth is simple, and so is life. It's us who are making it a greater deal than it actually is.

-This is it! We're at the tenth and final affirmation for the day. Breathe in through the nose. Breathe out through the nose. Let's listen in carefully to this final one.

-**"It is always the simple that produces the marvelous."** One more time. **"It is always the simple that produces the marvelous."**

-PAUSE FOR 10 SECONDS-

-No matter what you do in life, you have to keep simplicity a main core aspect of things. Complicating things will only result in more complications. Simplifying things will lead to great innovations, better lives, and greater productivity. Everything that is now great in the world has started with a simple idea. You built upon the simple, you keep it simple, and it becomes marvelous in the end naturally.

-Perfectly done! Wow, that was an excellent road for us to walk today, wasn't it? I know you might be sore or uneasy now, but all I'm asking from you is to bear with me until the end of the practice.

-You should be feeling great on the inside, having a clean, enhanced mind and a fluent body. Although, naturally, your legs or back might hurt a little if this is your first time sitting still for meditation. Perfectly normal reaction.

-We have now reached the final part of this practice. Now, it is time to get back to the bodily senses and take this minimalism meditation session to a close.

-Breathing in and out through the nose, use your sense of touch to feel the weight of the body pressing down in your chair or on the floor. Really feel the way the body interacts with the surface beneath it.

-Breathing in and out through the nose, use your sense of hearing to listen for any sounds in the room or outside of it. Try and notice sounds that are close to you, but also sounds that may come from the street outside.

-Breathing in and out through the nose, use your sense of taste and smell to see if you can notice any tastes in your mouth or any smells coming from around you.

-And finally, breathing in and out through the nose, gently open the eyes, and use the sense of sight to come back from the meditation completely. Take a second to appreciate this momentary freedom from thought and emotion, this complete bliss of body and mind.

-I want you to remember to take this feeling of calm and decluttering with you all throughout the day today in all of your activities today. Stay calm and gentle to your thoughts, emotions, and surroundings. Be good and keep things simple. Thank you!

Session #2 - For Your Child

-Welcome to today's meditation session. During this practice, we will explore together the power of the mind and the ways in which you can declutter the thoughts and feelings that sometimes overwhelm you as a kid or a teenager.

-As we begin to explore the depths of the mind today, all you have to do is to listen to this recording and try to follow the most of it, either by carefully listening or by following it directly and doing it with me.

-The first thing you have to do is to notice your breathing. If you want, you can simply listen to the practice while doing whatever it is that you're doing. It will still be effective. You can be on the train, doing homework, drawing, playing, or any other activity that can allow you to listen to this meditation. If you're at home, the best thing you can do is to sit comfortably in a still spot.

-Once you've sat down, what I want you to do is to start noticing your breathing for a few moments. Simply notice how the body moves as you breathe in through the nose and then exhale through the mouth. Once more, breathe in through the nose, feeling the way the chest expands, and then breathe out through the mouth, as the chest compresses back to its natural state.

-Great job. Now that you've started noticing the breath, you will have to keep a gentle focus on the breathing all throughout the practice. Whenever you feel like your focus is getting out of hand, simply bring everything back to the breath.

-Whatever it is that you do right now, we will move on into connecting with the mind and body for a better decluttering of both of them. Minimalism teaches us that a calm body and mind start with a clean life, house, car, or even room. For this to happen, we will focus on how the body can be decluttered by following a simple set of instructions.

-Begin with observing the entire body at first. Notice how the body feels right at this very moment. Don't be judgmental about it. If it's early morning when you listen to this meditation, your body might still be half asleep and colder. If it's late at night, the body might feel tired, painful, uneasy. Again, simply notice the general way the body feels right now.

126

-Next, let's focus on the pain points that you can feel right now in the body. Where is the body hurting right now? Are the knees hurting? Is the head experiencing any uncomfortable states? Do you feel any discomfort in the neck, back, chest area? Simply scan the body up and down and see if there's any pain anywhere on the body.

-Remember to breathe in and out through the nose and gently keep a focus on the breath while you do everything in this practice.

-Now we will be focusing on any tensions in the body. Scanning up and down the body, notice if you feel any tension anywhere on the body. Is there any tension in the legs or arms? Do you feel any tension in the back or abdomen? Wherever you might feel the discomfort, simply notice the tension, and then do absolutely nothing about it. Noticing it makes it go away naturally.

-The final scan for the day is for the purpose of finding the pleasure points of the body. Focusing on the positive, not just the negative, will make it possible for you to always find the good in any situation, which is an excellent way to learn minimalism in general.

-As you scan the body up and down, really try and focus on those areas of the body that are simply pleasant right now. They can feel calm, relaxed, easy. Uneventful. Simple. Those areas of the body are pleasure areas or points. Notice these points and take them into account, but don't try to do anything about them. Simply notice one, and then move on to the next.

-You are doing wonderfully. Remember, always bring your awareness back to the breath every time you feel like you're about to slip into the depths of unconscious thinking. Once you go for that uncontrolled thinking pattern, notice the breathing, and you'll immediately get yourself back to the moment and into the session.

-It is now time to better incorporate the idea of minimalism into the mind. The most important concepts of the ideology of minimalism are centered around thinking clearly in a safe, clutter-free environment. Healthy thinking goes hand in hand with a healthy home, school and playground. Start with your room and declutter the space you're spending the most time in. Help your family do the same with the living room, the kitchen, and the bathroom.

-The best way for us to practically implement the most useful ideas of minimalism into our lives is by listening to a series of powerful affirmations about it. These affirmations will help us better understand minimalism and how we can implement it into our lives. Before and after each affirmation, we will take a few big, deep breaths in through the nose and out through the mouth. Then, we will listen to some of the smartest people that ever lived teaching the art of minimalist living. Get ready. We will begin right now.

-Breathe in through the nose for 4 seconds. Focus on the fullness of the breath for a second. Breathe out for 5 seconds, and listen carefully.

-One: All that we are is the result of what we have thought. The mind is everything. What we think we become. One more time. **All that we are is the result of what we have thought. The mind is everything. What we think we become.**

-Breathe in through the nose for 4 seconds. Focus on the fullness of the breath for a second. Breathe out for 5 seconds, and listen carefully.

-All negativity arises because of mind. If the mind is transformed, negativity never remains. Again. **All negativity arises because of mind. If the mind is transformed, negativity never remains.**

-Breathe in through the nose for 4 seconds. Focus on the fullness of the breath for a second. Breathe out for 5 seconds, and listen carefully.

-However many holy words you read, however many you speak, no good will they do you If you do not act upon them. Once more. **However many holy words you read, however many you speak, no good will they do you If you do not act upon them.**

-Breathe in through the nose for 4 seconds. Focus on the fullness of the breath for a second. Breathe out for 5 seconds, and listen carefully.

-Do not dwell in the past, do not dream of the future, concentrate the mind on the present moment. Again. **Do not dwell in the past, do not dream of the future, concentrate the mind on the present**

128

moment.

-Breathe in through the nose for 4 seconds. Focus on the fullness of the breath for a second. Breathe out for 5 seconds, and listen carefully.

-In the sky, there is no distinction between **east and west; people create distinctions out of their own minds and then believe them to be true.** One more time. **In the sky, there is no distinction of east and west; people create distinctions out of their own minds and then believe them to be true.**

-Breathe in through the nose for 4 seconds. Focus on the fullness of the breath for a second. Breathe out for 5 seconds, and listen carefully.

-Amazing, you have been doing great. In this short break, we will once again pay attention to the breathing. Remembering that all of your life, from the moment of your birth, and all the way to this very moment, has been, is, and will be nothing but a series of breaths. Between each inhale and exhale happens the entirety of your life.

-The act of breathing, while simple, is the most important way to reconnect with your body and experience life as it is. Simply breathing will solve most of your everyday problems because breathing gets you back to the present moment, while most of your difficulties focus your attention in the past or the future. Both of which do not exist between two breaths.

-We will now be focusing on a series of affirmations that will help you deal with the uncertainty and the novelty of turning to a minimalist life as a kid or teenager. We will listen to these affirmations twice for each one of them, focusing on the breath while we do so.

-After we listen to the affirmation, we'll move to a small break where you will be able to fully grasp the meaning of it, then talk about it in a few words to completely understand the message behind each and every one of them. Get ready, as we're about to begin.

--READ THE AFFIRMATIONS SLOWLY, CLEARLY AND EASILY --

-Okay, here's the first affirmation for the day. Listen to it carefully while keeping a gentle focus on the breath. Let the mind be, but focus on the inhale and exhale when you get lost.

-I love and approve of myself. I feel the love of those who are not physically around me. Once more. **I love and approve of myself. I feel the love of those who are not physically around me.**

-PAUSE FOR 10 SECONDS-

-Nice! Love doesn't have to go both ways. Understanding true love, the simple act of unconditional love, means understanding that loving yourself and the ones around you starts with you. It doesn't have to be both ways, you don't have to wait for a reward to love another human being. And you should love yourself even when you feel down or sad.

-The second affirmation is now ready for us to listen to. While doing so, remember to gently focus your mind to the breath. This will help you better align with the message of this one.

-I focus on breathing and grounding myself. Following my intuition and my heart keeps me safe and sound. Again. **I focus on breathing and grounding myself. Following my intuition and my heart keeps me safe and sound.**

-PAUSE FOR 10 SECONDS-

-Most people look for answers about staying put and at ease with the crazy world around them in books. But books never have to teach you the most basic aspects of life. You were born knowing right from wrong. Follow your breathing, your heart and intuition, and you'll be kept away from harm.

-Here comes the third meditative affirmation of this practice today. As we know by now, we'll be focusing on the breathing, as well as on letting these great words of wisdom flow into our mind.

-I have as much brightness to offer the world as the next person. Once more. **I have as much brightness to offer the world as the next person.**

-PAUSE FOR 10 SECONDS-

Good job! When people are measuring themselves in comparison to others, they usually refer to things like money, fame, social status or anything else that's material. Instead of doing so, living a minimalist life means measuring ourselves in terms of how much joy and blissfulness we have and not comparing ourselves to others.

-Next, we'll be focusing on the fourth affirmation of this series. Get ready for this new one as you follow the breath which is now gentle, effortless, calm and easy. Let's listen in.

-I trust my inner wisdom and intuition. Wonderful things unfold before me. Again. **I trust my inner wisdom and intuition. Wonderful things unfold before me.**

-PAUSE FOR 10 SECONDS-

-Nice! The best thing you can do when you have to make an important decision to listen deep within you. You can learn from others and consult with them but trust yourself to know what is right for you. Open up to your inside being, listen to your own wisdom and intuition. They will guide you towards a better decision in all of the cases. When this happens, it is natural that amazing things will unfold.

-Here's the fifth and final affirmation of this first part. We'll take a short break after this one, but until then, let's listen in to these following words of great wisdom. Here they come now.

-I forgive myself for all the mistakes I have made. Once more. **I forgive myself for all the mistakes I have made.**

-PAUSE FOR 10 SECONDS-

-Good! Forgiving can't happen from you to others unless a very important step has been taken. And that is, you forgiving yourself for all of the things that you've done wrong. You can start small, as we all know that the hardest critic that we have is ourselves. Start by forgiving yourself for a bad thought that you've had for a while. Built upon that compassion. Grow into a forgiver.

131

-Excellent, you've done great thus far and it is now time to reward that with a small break in which you can relax your body and your mind. Gently shake off any tension that might've built up in the muscles, joints, legs or arms. Turn the neck around to shake off any cramps in there. Let the body breathe, as well as the mind rest. Perfect.

-PAUSE FOR 10 SECONDS-

-Let's move along now. Here's affirmation number six for you today. We'll again listen to it carefully and gently follow our breath as a guide for the entire experience. Here it goes.

-I replace my anger with understanding and compassion. Again. **I replace my anger with understanding and compassion.**

-PAUSE FOR 10 SECONDS-

-Awesome! Why should we replace an angry thought or action with compassion? Why should we respond to a conflict with calm and understanding? Because it's not in our nature to become agitated over most things. We should only be defensive if it really is necessary to become like that. Most of the time though, letting anger go is 100% better than responding to it with more anger. Let it go, understand, and show compassion. It's priceless.

-As we move closer and closer to the end of this practice, we've now reached the seventh affirmation of the day. This one is about choices, minimalist choices for a better life. Listen.

-I choose to find hopeful and optimistic ways to look at every situation. Once more. **I choose to find hopeful and optimistic ways to look at every situation.**

-PAUSE FOR 10 SECONDS-

-Making the right choice is critical, regardless if we're dealing with a small or a big situation in life. How do we make the right choices though? It's simple. We don't overcrowd our options. We keep a steady eye on hope and optimism, and sort through the possible outcomes of any situation with a clear mind and good control of it. If there's no choice for these at all, we're clearly in the wrong situation and should stay away from anything having to do with it.

-Our eight affirmation is now here so, as with the rest of them, let's listen in carefully. Keep a gentle focus on your breathing. It should now be steady, calm, effortless.

- I listen lovingly to this inner conflict and reflect on it until I find peace around it. Again. **I listen lovingly to this inner conflict and reflect on it until I find peace around it.**

-PAUSE FOR 10 SECONDS-

Inner conflicts are more often than not bigger than outside ones. You can fight with your arms and legs when confronted in a physical situation. But when the conflict is on the inside, no arms, no legs, no matter how strong, are going to be able to help you. Fighting with your mind is impossible. Listening to it, though, is a noble, logical thing to do. The only way to ease an inner conflict is to listen and reflect. Peace will naturally come if you don't force things within.

-Nine affirmations down after this one, which means we're getting really close to the end. This one, you're going to like it for sure. Let's listen in and see what it says.

-My thoughts are my reality so I think up a bright new day. Today will be a gorgeous day to remember. Once more. **My thoughts are my reality so I think up a bright new day. Today will be a gorgeous day to remember.**

-PAUSE FOR 10 SECONDS-

-Wonderful. Buddha used to say that we become exactly what we think. If we think we'll be happy, we will be happy. Thoughts, these unseen bolts of electricity in our brains, ultimately become our reality. If you start each day on a positive note, thinking about how bright of a life you'll live for the next 24 hours, you will create the day you wish to remember for yourself over that period of time.

-And now, as we move close to the end of the practice, let's listen to the tenth and final affirmation of the day. Listen carefully to this final

133

one, breathing gently in and out through the nose.

-Having more won't solve the problem. Happiness does not lie in possessions. The answer lies within. Again. **Having more won't solve the problem. Happiness does not lie in possessions. The answer lies within.**

-PAUSE FOR 10 SECONDS-

-Superb! The ultimate truth about life and living it in a minimalist way is this: having more is never going to make you feel more, or happier. Having is never a problem solver. Possessions are frugal, which makes them temporary sources of happiness. Once a new product is out, you're again miserable for not having it. True happiness, the answer to life and all of its questions, will only be found if you look within yourself.

-What a positive way to view life through these affirmations that have now become part of yourself. Remember to always look for these affirmations in your mind whenever you're faced with a disruptive situation. Whenever you feel lost, down or uneasy, all you have to do is to search deep within you for these sentences, which may appear general and common at first, but have a powerful effect on all those who take them for what they truly are.

-As we move closer to the end of our practice today, all I want you to do next is to step out of your meditative state and back into the real world. you may now start your journey back to the present time.

-Engage your sense of touch first. Feel the pressure points of the body touching the surface under it. Feel how the skin touches the clothes on you. Feel the weight of the hand and legs. Feel the Earth pulling you towards its center using the gravity.

-Next, turn on your sense of hearing. Listen for whatever sounds you might be hearing around you. They can be close sounds, like those coming from inside of your room, or they can be sounds from afar, like those coming out from the street.

-Finally, engage the sense of sight by gently opening your eyes, taking a

134

deep breath and enjoying the peacefulness and calm. Take a moment to congratulate yourself on sitting down and saying yes to the meditative practice today. Reassuring yourself that from now on, you're a better minimalist, an understanding and patient child and family member.

-Make sure you'll put in the effort to keep yourself this way today, tomorrow, and for the days ahead. Responding to uncertainty with calm. To stress with relaxation. And to dispute with compassion and pleasure. Being more and more aware of just how important it is to be living with less, rather than with more.

-About how easy it is to be put in a situation where having less is a blessing. Just how simple it is to organize everything when they're truly the things that you need. When you find the power to do this, you will make your way from a simple living, to a complex living with close to nothing.

-This is the ultimate power of your own decision. Decide to live more, with less.

-Thank you for taking the time to listen to this practice today. Enjoy the benefits of sitting down and being at ease with your thoughts, feelings and emotions for the past hour or so. May you find calm in whatever it is that you're about to do for the next few hours.

-Have a peaceful day.

Before we part, I would like to once again remind you that as a self-publishing author, reviews are the lifeblood of my work. I would be very happy and thankful if you could take a few moments to leave a review on Amazon. I truly appreciate your time.

REFERENCES

5 Everyday Minimalist Habits to Adopt Right Now. (2019). Retrieved from https://www.arcido.com/blogs/news/5-everyday-minimalist-habits-to-adopt-right-now

7 tips for dealing with change. (n.d.). Retrieved from https://au.reachout.com/articles/7-tips-for-dealing-with-change

8 Easy Ways To Become A Minimalist. (2018). Retrieved from https://makespace.com/blog/posts/how-to-become-a-minimalist/

Aitchison, S. (2017). 5 Reasons Why Less Is More. Retrieved from https://www.stevenaitchison.co.uk/5-reasons-less/

Aknina, L. B., Nortonband , M. I., & Dunn, E. W. (2009). From wealth to well-being? Money matters, but less than people think. Retrieved from https://www.hbs.edu/faculty/Publication Files/aknin norton dunn from wealth to well being_b0ba361d-d6f6-493b-b99a-633d93f14f7c.pdf

Babauta, L. (n.d.). zen habits. Retrieved from https://zenhabits.net/a-guide-to-creating-a-minimalist-home/

Babauta, L. (n.d.). zen habits. Retrieved from https://zenhabits.net/minimal-kids/

Barahona, D. (2019). How to Parent Like a Minimalist. Retrieved from https://nosidebar.com/minimalist-parenting/

Becker, J. (2014). Raising Consumer Conscious Teenagers in an Age of Excess. Retrieved from https://www.becomingminimalist.com/consumer-conscious-teens/

Becker, J. (2017). Lessons Learned From Intentionally Letting Go. Retrieved from https://www.becomingminimalist.com/let-it-go/

Becker, J. (2019). 4 Ways Minimalism Can Improve Parenting. Retrieved from https://www.becomingminimalist.com/own-less-parent-better/

Becker, J. (2019). 7 Common Problems Solved by Owning Less Stuff. Retrieved from https://www.becomingminimalist.com/7-common-problems-solved-by-owning-less/

Becker, J. (2019). 9 Reasons Buying Stuff Will Never Make You Happy. Retrieved from https://www.becomingminimalist.com/buying-stuff-wont-make-you-happy/

Becker, J. (2019). 10 Positive Psychology Studies to Change Your View of Happiness. Retrieved from https://www.becomingminimalist.com/happier/

Becker, J. (2019). 10 Reasons Why Minimalism is Growing. Retrieved from https://www.becomingminimalist.com/10-reasons-why-minimalism-is-growing-a-k-a-10-reasons-you-should-adopt-the-lifestyle/

Becker, J. (2019). How to Declutter Your Home: 10 Creative Decluttering Tips. Retrieved from https://www.becomingminimalist.com/creative-ways-to-declutter/

Becker, J. (2019). What Is Minimalism? Retrieved from https://www.becomingminimalist.com/what-is-minimalism/

Becker, J. (2019). Why Minimalism Should Not Be Entered Into Lightly. Retrieved from https://www.becomingminimalist.com/why-minimalism-should-not-be-entered-into-lightly/

Becker, J. (n.d.). How to Become Minimalist with Children. Retrieved from https://www.becomingminimalist.com/how-to-become-minimalist-with-children/

Browne, K. (2015). Organize Your Bedroom: A Step-By-Step Guide For Teenagers. Retrieved from https://www.getorganizedwizard.com/blog/2015/02/organize-bedroom-step-step-guide-teenagers/

Buying Experiences, Not Possessions, Leads To Greater Happiness. (2009). Retrieved from https://www.sciencedaily.com/releases/2009/02/090207150518.htm

Cardenas, A. (2018). When Parents Fail Their Own Children. Retrieved from https://exploringyourmind.com/parents-fail-their-own-children/

Carroll, S. (n.d.). 5 tips to make minimalism work for your family. Retrieved from https://www.focusonthefamily.ca/content/5-tips-to-make-minimalism-work-for-your-family

Carver, C. (2017). Notes From a Minimalist Teen. Retrieved from https://bemorewithless.com/notes-from-a-minimalist-teen/

Carver, C. (2019). 7 Tiny Steps for the Beginner Minimalist. Retrieved from https://bemorewithless.com/begin/

Carver, C. (2020). Minimalism for Families: the do's and don'ts of simplifying together. Retrieved from https://bemorewithless.com/minimalism-for-families/

Chalk, C. (2019). Striving for Digital Minimalism: Why We Need a Human-Centric Approach to Technology. Retrieved from https://www.thepublicdiscourse.com/2019/04/50540/

Clear, J. (2015). Stop Thinking and Start Doing: The Power of Practicing More. Retrieved from https://lifehacker.com/stop-thinking-and-start-doing-the-power-of-practicing-1694073303

Danielle, M. (2019). The History of Minimalism And What Minimalism Means as a Lifestyle. Retrieved from https://miadanielle.com/what-is-minimalism/

Davison, B. (2018). Little Changes To Your Home That Can Reduce Your Stress. Retrieved from https://www.housebeautiful.com/lifestyle/g23876460/design-mistakes-stressful-home/

Digital Detox And A Simple Life Of Minimalism. (2019). Retrieved from https://minimalistboy.com/digital-detox/

Digital Minimalism: Give Me Back My Brain. (2019). Retrieved from https://clippingchains.com/2019/06/10/digital-minimalism-give-me-back-my-brain/

Digital Minimalism: my digital detox experience. (2019). Retrieved from https://www.reddit.com/r/minimalism/comments/b9p3vl/digital_minimalism_my_digital_detox_experience/

Druecke, G. (n.d.). How to Create a Minimalist Home Without Throwing Everything Away. Retrieved from https://thebalimarket.us/blogs/turkishtowels/create-a-minimalist-home

Durmonski, I. (2019). The 11 Best Minimalism Tips That Will Help You Stay a Minimalist. Retrieved from https://durmonski.com/minimalism/the-11-best-minimalism-tips/

Elmore, T. (2016). Three Reasons for Teen Unhappiness and What to Do About It. Retrieved from https://www.psychologytoday.com/us/blog/artificial-maturity/201610/three-reasons-teen-unhappiness-and-what-do-about-it

Espiritu, D. (2017). Why We Often Struggle With Material Things. Retrieved from https://www.dhennespiritu.com/struggle-with-material-things/

Esposito, L. (2016). Minimalism: When Living With Less Means More Mental Health. Retrieved from https://www.psychologytoday.com/us/blog/anxiety-

zen/201612/minimalism-when-living-less-means-more-mental-
health

Estrada, J. (2019). 5 Mindful Habits that Lead to a Minimalist Home.
Retrieved from https://www.apartmenttherapy.com/5-mindful-
habits-that-lead-to-a-minimalist-home-238768

Family & Relationship Problems. (n.d.). Retrieved from
https://www.lifeline.org.au/get-help/topics/family-relationship-
problems

Family common problems. (n.d.). Retrieved from
https://www.relate.org.uk/relationship-help/help-family-life-and-
parenting/family-common-problems

Fechter, J. (2015). Less Is More: 19 Reasons Being A Minimalist Is The
Best Way Of Life. Retrieved from
https://www.elitedaily.com/life/motivation/19-reasons-becoming-
minimalist-best-choice-youll-ever-make/888733

Feindt , J. (n.d.). Minimalism: Having Less Gives You More. Retrieved
from https://patients.scnm.edu/blog/minimalism-having-less-
gives-you-more~2661

Fessler, P. (2016). Living From Rent To Rent: Tenants On The Edge
Of Eviction. Retrieved from
https://www.npr.org/2016/03/29/471347542/living-from-rent-to-
rent-tenants-on-the-edge-of-eviction?t=1579768205149

Fisk, L. (2019). 9 Surprisingly Simple Minimalist Habits That Will
Enhance Your Life. Retrieved from
https://simplequietmama.com/minimalist-habits-that-will-enhance-
your-life/

Florio, G. M. (2016). 7 Ways Your Home Life Could Be Giving You
Anxiety. Retrieved from https://www.bustle.com/articles/167516-
7-ways-your-home-life-could-be-giving-you-anxiety

Frank, R. (2011). Don't Envy the Super-Rich, They Are Miserable.
Retrieved from https://blogs.wsj.com/wealth/2011/03/09/dont-

envy-the-super-rich-they-are-miserable/

Garner, C. (2018). Digital mental health: the rise and struggle of mental health games. Retrieved from https://www.scitecheuropa.eu/digital-mental-health-games/90767/

Gardner, B. (2019). Why Minimalism is a Better Way of Life. Retrieved from https://nosidebar.com/why-minimalism/

Gardner, B. (2019). Why Minimalism is a Better Way of Life. Retrieved from https://nosidebar.com/why-minimalism/

Gottschalk-Scher, L. (2014). Raising Minimalist Children in a Modern World. Retrieved from https://www.everydayfamily.com/raising-minimalist-children-in-a-modern-world/

Greenberg, B. (2016). 10 Reasons Why People Get Cut Off From Their Family. Retrieved from https://www.psychologytoday.com/us/blog/the-teen-doctor/201707/10-reasons-why-people-get-cut-their-family

Having vs Doing vs Being and the Meaning of Life. (n.d.). Retrieved from https://topyogis.com/blog/philosophy/having-vs-doing-vs-being-and-meaning-life

Hazlewood, L. (2019). Stop the Madness: 6 Expert Tips on How to Declutter Your Makeup Collection. Retrieved from https://fashionmagazine.com/face-body/tips-on-how-to-declutter-your-makeup/

Henson, B. (2019). Meet The Minimalist: Amanda. Retrieved from https://somedayslower.com/meettheminimalistamamda

Herd, C. (2019). Why Digital Minimalism could be the Key to Improving your Mental Health. Retrieved from https://medium.com/@ChrisHerd/why-digital-minimalism-could-be-the-key-to-improving-your-mental-health-e5fcd85c9763

How To Be A Minimalist With A Family - BEFORE AND AFTER MINIMALISM. (2019). Retrieved from https://shannontorrens.com/how-to-be-a-minimalist-with-a-family-before-and-after-minimalism-become-more-minimal-as-a-family-of-4/

How to Get Your Family On Board With Minimalism. (2019). Retrieved from https://www.simplyfiercely.com/how-to-get-your-family-on-board-with-minimalism/

How to implement minimalism in your everyday life. (2018). Retrieved from https://stop-the-water-while-using-me.com/en/blog/how-to-implement-minimalism-in-your-everyday-life

How To Simplify Your Life Now To Find Bliss " According To Malin. (2019). Retrieved from https://accordingtomalin.com/how-to-simplify-your-life-now-to-find-bliss/

I'm Not Busy (And I'm Proud of It). (2018). Retrieved from https://www.theminimalistmom.com/notbusy/

Is Your Home Stressing You Out? (2018). Retrieved from https://cedarhillfarmhouse.com/is-your-home-stressing-you-out/

Jones, R. (2019). Everything You Ever Wanted to Know About Minimalism. Retrieved from https://nourishingminimalism.com/know-minimalism/

Kaplan, J. (2019). 7 Reasons to Declutter Right Now. Retrieved from https://www.thespruce.com/reasons-to-declutter-right-now-4140438

Kim, Z. (2019). A Guide to Let Go of Your Perfectly Good Things. Retrieved from https://www.becomingminimalist.com/letting-go/

Kim , Z. (2019). Why Families Need Minimalism. Retrieved from https://www.becomingminimalist.com/families-need-minimalism/

Kim, Z. (2019). A Practical Guide to Minimalism with Kids. Retrieved from https://nosidebar.com/minimalism-with-kids/

Koh, C., & Dornfest, A. (n.d.). 6 Steps to Minimalist Parenting. Retrieved from https://www.parenting.com/pregnancy/planning/minimalist-parenting/

Kos, B. (2017). Everything you need to know about minimalism as the coolest lifestyle. Retrieved from https://agileleanlife.com/minimalism/

Kowalski, K. (2019). Digital Minimalism Defined & 10 Digital Declutter Tips. Retrieved from https://www.sloww.co/digital-minimalism/

Lambrecht, C. (2019). Retrieved from https://www.calnewport.com/blog/2019/03/01/digital-minimalism-for-parents/

Landis, J. (2019). 5 Ways Millennial Parents Can Add Minimalism to Their Homes. Retrieved from https://www.verywellfamily.com/why-millennial-parents-embrace-minimalism-4136641

Less is more: 10 practical ways to be minimalist. (2017). Retrieved from https://medium.com/@milenarangelov/10-ways-less-is-more-f61a070a65c3

Marie Kondo: The Japanese Art of Decluttering and Organizing. (2019). Retrieved from https://fs.blog/2014/12/the-life-changing-magic-of-tidying-up/

Minimal Living Will Make Your Life Better. (2016). Retrieved from https://themerrymakersisters.com/minimal-living/

Minimalism Before And After: How It Changed My Life. (2019). Retrieved from https://www.simplyfiercely.com/minimalism-changed-life/

Minimalism Do's and Dont's. (2019). Retrieved from https://www.simplyfiercely.com/minimalism-dos-and-donts/

Minimalist Parenting Tips To Decrease Stress & Increase Fun! (2018). Retrieved from https://musthavemom.com/minimalist-parenting-tips-decrease-stress/

Minimalist: When Your Family is Not. (2016). Retrieved from https://www.raisingsimple.com/minimalist-when-your-family-is-not/

Murray, C., Murray, C., Murray, C., & Murray, C. (2020). Minimalist Living: How Can It Benefit Your Life Significantly. Retrieved from https://www.moneyunder30.com/minimalist-living

Nicodemus, R. (2019). What Is Minimalism? Retrieved from https://www.theminimalists.com/minimalism/

Nicodemus, R., & Millburn , J. F. (2020). Learning to Let Go. Retrieved from https://www.theminimalists.com/letgo/

Ngo, K.-N. (2019). 5 Tips for Being a Teenage Minimalist. Retrieved from https://www.eightpercenthuman.com/home/2019/3/5/being-a-teenage-minimalist

Ofei, M. (2018). What Is Minimalism? An Introduction To Living With Intentionality. Retrieved from https://theminimalistvegan.com/what-is-minimalism/

Ongaro, A. (2018). 10 Simple Minimalism Guidelines. Retrieved from https://www.breakthetwitch.com/minimalism-guidelines/

Oppong, T. (2016). The "Do Something" Mindset (The Power of Practicing More). Retrieved from https://medium.com/the-mission/the-do-something-mindset-the-power-of-practicing-more-883d62a3b2a4

Penner, E. (2019). How We Embrace Minimalism with Kids. Retrieved from https://modernminimalism.com/how-we-embrace-minimalism-with-kids/

Peduzzi, M. (2019). 10 Ways of Creating Family Connections for Building Strong Bonds. Retrieved from https://www.aha-now.com/creating-family-connections/

Philipp, C. (2019). How Digital Minimalism Can Help You Reclaim Your Time and Your Life. Retrieved from https://www.theepochtimes.com/how-digital-minimalism-can-help-you-reclaim-your-time-and-your-life_2855997.html

Relojo-Howell, D. (2018). How Consumerism Affects Our Well-being. Retrieved from https://www.psychreg.org/consumerism-well-being/

Santos, A. (2019). How Minimalist Principles Can Help You In Your Relationship. Retrieved from https://thriveglobal.com/stories/how-minimalist-principles-can-help-you-in-your-relationship/

Shliakhau, R. (2016). How to Stay a Minimalist. Retrieved from https://nosidebar.com/stay-minimalist/

Silvestre, D. (2019). Minimalist Living: How to Lead a More Frugal Life. Retrieved from https://dansilvestre.com/minimalist-living/

Strebe, S. (2019). My Design Style Is Simple-This Is How I Create a Minimal Interior. Retrieved from https://www.mydomaine.com/minimalist-interior-design

Summers, C. (2015). 8 Lessons Our Editor Learned from the Decluttering Bible. Retrieved from https://www.onekingslane.com/live-love-home/marie-kondo-book-declutter/

The Minimalists. (2020). Retrieved from https://en.wikipedia.org/wiki/The_Minimalists

Tritt, J. (2019). Minimalism and Relationships. Retrieved from https://nosidebar.com/relationships/

Wallen, D. (2013). 7 Reasons Why Materialistic Stuff Doesn't Lead To Happiness. Retrieved from https://www.lifehack.org/articles/communication/7-reasons-why-materialistic-stuff-doesnt-lead-happiness.html

Wells, K. (2018). Minimalism With a Family (Benefits & How to Do It): Wellness Mama. Retrieved from https://wellnessmama.com/344224/minimalism/

What is Minimalism? Plus 8 Things it's NOT. (2019). Retrieved from https://simplelionheartlife.com/what-is-minimalism/

Why & How to Embrace Minimalist Parenting. (2019). Retrieved from https://www.greenchildmagazine.com/minimalist-parenting/

Why Families Need Minimalism. (2019). Retrieved from https://www.becomingminimalist.com/families-need-minimalism/

Why Kids Need Minimalism. (2019). Retrieved from https://www.becomingminimalist.com/kids-need-minimalism/

Williams-Burris, S. (2020). 14 Common Family Problems: How to Cope Without Losing Your Sanity. Retrieved from http://lifestyleprowess.com/common-family-problems/